Nobody Came

Nobody Came

The appalling true story of brothers cruelly
abused in a Jersey care home

Robbie Garner

with Toni Maguire

HarperElement
An Imprint of HarperCollins*Publishers*
77–85 Fulham Palace Road,
Hammersmith, London W6 8JB

www.harpercollins.co.uk

and *HarperElement* are trademarks
of HarperCollins*Publishers* Ltd

First published by HarperElement 2008
2

© Robbie Garner 2008

Robbie Garner asserts the moral right to
be identified as the author of this work

A catalogue record of this book is
available from the British Library

HB ISBN-13 978-0-00-728794-9
PB ISBN-13 978-0-00-728795-6

Printed and bound in Great Britain by
Clays Ltd, St Ives plc

Mixed Sources
Product group from well-managed
forests and other controlled sources
www.fsc.org   Cert no. SW-COC-1806
© 1996 Forest Stewardship Council

FSC is a non-profit international organisation established to promote the
responsible management of the world's forests. Products carrying the FSC
label are independently certified to assure consumers that they come
from forests that are managed to meet the social, economic and
ecological needs of present and future generations.

Find out more about HarperCollins and the environment at
www.harpercollins.co.uk/green

Acknowledgements

Special thanks to Barbara Levy, and her assistant Vicki Salter; to Gill Paul; and to Carole Tonkinson and all the team at HarperCollins.

Prologue

I'm an ordinary man; maybe some people would call me an insignificant one. I don't mind if they do. I know who I am.

I like order in my life; routine is important to me. It's that everyday sameness that has at last given me peace. Each morning before I leave my house I make my bed the way I was made to do as a boy: sheets pulled up tightly and the corners tucked in neatly. I wash my mug and plate and place them in the cupboard over the sink. And when I return home from work it's my practice to take a shower, pull on jeans and a T-shirt, put away my work clothes and make a mug of tea just in time to watch the evening news.

But it was that very routine that destroyed the calmness in my life. The calmness that had taken me so many years to achieve disappeared on a February night when I turned on my television and heard the words 'abuse, rape and cover-up'.

It was the newsreader informing viewers that the dark side of Jersey had been exposed.

Suddenly the screen was filled with the blown-up photograph of a large granite building; a building that I, with a rising feeling of nausea, immediately recognised – Haut de la Garenne. Then the picture changed to show dogs on leashes held by white-coated handlers. The police had brought in sniffer dogs.

The remains of a child had been found, they said.

'Only one?' I thought to myself.

The camera moved on to a young reporter standing in the grounds who, with a sympathetic expression on his face and a microphone in his hand, was addressing his unseen audience of millions.

'The secrets and lies of Jersey have finally come to light,' he told us. 'What has been revealed has shocked the residents of an island known not just for its beauty, but also for its tranquillity and lack of crime.'

'Behind me,' the reporter's voice continued, 'is the children's home where, over a period of nearly ten decades, more than a thousand youngsters have been fed, clothed and housed by the charity of Jersey's government.

'Some were orphans, some were abandoned, others had been taken into care, but whatever the reason they had been placed in this grey Victorian building they all had one thing in common – vulnerability. They, more than any others, were in need of love, understanding and protection. However, here that was denied them; for it was in this institution that their childhood lost its final struggle to exist.'

The picture changed again and we were back with the newsreader, who informed us that the complaints, the allegations and the whispered stories that had rebounded over Jersey for nearly half a century had finally come to be investigated. Those rumours of rape, torture and even worse had now become shocking accusations.

He said the police feared there might be more human remains buried in six other suspect sites the dogs had found. In the cellars underneath the main building a room showed signs that it had been used as a torture chamber. Over a hundred adults, who had once been the children of Haut de la Garenne, had made accusation after accusation to Jersey's police of the abuse that allegedly had taken place there. In fact, one of those people was in the studio.

The camera swung round to focus on an elderly couple that the newsreader was about to interview. The husband, a decade or more older than me, was in a wheelchair. His wife sat next to him, her hand resting lightly on his arm. I could clearly see the tremor in his age-spotted hands as he prepared himself for the questions he knew were going to be put to him.

His first answer was bleak and simple. 'Yes, I was there,' he said. 'I was at that place.'

As the words left his mouth, his chin trembled and tears leaked from his eyes. And putting my hand to my face I found corresponding tears had dampened my cheeks; the tears of the smooth-skinned boy I had once been.

And the only thought filling my head then was: and so was I.

Chapter One

Once the initial shock of hearing the words 'Haut de la Garenne' had faded I tried to make my mind travel back in time and revisit the past. I knew that I wouldn't be able to leave my childhood memories buried any longer. The relentless surge of interest in Jersey's secrets would make sure of that. But I'd kept my thoughts so carefully concealed for so long that they refused to obey me. I couldn't think about either the granite building that dominated the news or the orphanage, run by the nuns, which I had been sent to first. 'Not yet,' they said to me, 'not yet.' Instead they bypassed that time and went straight back to that last summer I spent with my family. The summer before they took us away.

Six of us – my mother, Stanley (her current man), my two brothers, me, and the latest addition to our family, a baby sister – lived in Devonshire Place in St Helier, the capital of Jersey. It was an unremarkable area made up of terraced houses, a couple of pubs and a few corner shops. A place where families lived, children played and women stood on their doorsteps, cigarette smoke swirling around their heads, swapping gossip with the neighbours. A street like many others; certainly there was nothing unusual about it, but in summer, when the sun shone on the pastel-painted houses, I thought it was pretty. And it was my home.

We all lived in three rooms on the top floor of one of those houses. Directly beneath the uninsulated roof, they were cold and draughty in winter but stuffy and airless in summer.

I was the middle boy. My elder brother John, with his spiky blond hair that refused to obey his brush however much he dampened it, his wide impish grin and his infectious laugh, was eight, three years older than me.

Davie, the youngest, with his round little stomach and chubby legs and indentations on either side of his mouth, was all curves and dimples. He had just learnt to talk in partial sentences and with a wide grin on his pink-cheeked face claimed our attention by chattering to us as fast as he could. He followed John and me around our rooms, stumbling in his haste, his legs slightly bowed, for at three he was still in bulky towelling nappies; not so much because he couldn't tell one of us when he wanted a wee but because our mother didn't want to climb down three flights of stairs to the outside lavatory with him. Even sitting him on a potty regularly appeared to take too much effort. Davie often remained all day in his damp nappy until his eight-year-old brother came home from school and changed it.

I looked like neither of them. I had a slight frame, fine dark hair and grey eyes that peered myopically at the world.

John told me that he knew Stanley wasn't his father because he dimly remembered the time when he first came to live with Gloria. We always called her Gloria – never mum.

'You arrived soon after,' he told me. 'So I guess Stanley's your dad but he's not Davie's.'

'How do you know?' I asked in a puzzled voice, but John didn't answer me then.

Years later he told me that he'd overheard Stanley shouting at Gloria, asking her who the baby's father was, when he found out that she was pregnant with Davie. Certainly with his light brown hair and round face, he bore no resemblance to the dark-haired, olive-skinned Stanley, but Gloria insisted he could only be his. Denise was dark like Stanley but it was hard to tell what her baby features would be like when she grew up.

Another reason I always believed that Stanley was my father was that although he was mild-mannered and never said an unpleasant word to my brothers, it was me he seemed to single out for attention. Sometimes it was just a warm smile and a hand brushed lightly across my head. Occasionally, when Gloria was out of hearing range, he would fumble in his pocket, draw out a few coins and place them quickly in my hand.

'Buy yourself some sweets, lad,' he would whisper to me and I knew to hide the money away from Gloria's sharp gaze. He even on rare occasions took me down to the pier on the small wooden cart attached to his bicycle and treated me to an ice-cream. But apart from those few encounters he was rarely seen, nor did he involve himself with any of us.

Stanley was a landscape gardener who left for work early each morning, seven days a week, dressed smartly in caramel corduroy trousers and a brown tweed jacket, and returned late at night after we were in bed. The early start was no doubt because of the wish to get to work but the lateness of his return was, I would now guess, due to his reluctance to be in my mother's company.

On the other hand, Gloria left the rooms infrequently, apart from her visits to the hairdressers to have a perm or get her colour touched up. Her days were spent sipping gin mixed with lemonade, which she poured into a glass almost the moment she woke, while flicking through magazines like *Woman's Weekly* and *Woman's Realm*, painting her nails, plucking her eyebrows and winding her hair onto large pink plastic curlers.

She was someone who preferred to entertain her friends at home – mainly men, all of whom we were told to call uncle. They only came when Stanley was out at work.

I always knew by her languid preparations when these visitors were expected. Her long red hair was brushed into smooth waves, powder fluffed over her face, a small brush spat on then dipped in some sort of black goo before being applied to her eyelashes, and lastly red lipstick was smeared on a mouth she turned in then pushed out into a pout. Checking her teeth in the mirror for lipstick marks she would smile at herself knowingly. She was ready.

Watching these preparations, my little brother and I waited for what always came next. She turned to look at us as if she was seeing us for the first time, or as though she had forgotten our existence. When she noticed Davie and me gazing at her, the smile faded from her lips to be replaced by a look of irritation at our presence.

'Robbie,' she said to me each time, 'when my visitor arrives, say hello then take Davie into your room and keep him quiet. When John comes back from school I'll send him out for our supper. Trotters and chips, all right?'

Pigs' trotters, fried in bubbling fat until the skin was so crisp it looked like batter, was our favourite supper. Content with my bribe, I smiled, nodded and accepted the terms.

Often when the uncles arrived they would bring Davie and me a paper bag containing sticky toffees and sometimes even old copies of *Beano* or *Dandy* comics, clearly already read by other children.

'Thank you, sir,' I would say, for my mother had instilled in all of us the need for good manners towards the uncles, and clutching the booty I would push my baby brother into our room. We greedily stuffed the sweets into our mouths the moment the bedroom door was shut and then with bulging cheeks settled down to play. I couldn't read the comics so I put them on one side for John. He would either read them or invent stories to make the illustrations come alive later when we had finished our supper.

Making the appropriate 'woom, woom' sounds, we ran battered Dinky cars across the thin carpet, piled up painted wooden bricks, which Davie knocked down, then played with our wax crayons. I'd draw him pictures and he would chortle with laughter at my attempts. Matchstick figures of people appeared on paper, then I dressed and coloured them in, gave them a square house and finally drew in flowers and a tree.

But however much I concentrated on the games and my drawings, the walls were so thin that I could hear every sound coming from the sitting room. The gurgle of beer being poured, lemonade splashing into gin, the small screech of the gramophone needle when it was placed carelessly, with a drunk's lack of precision, onto the record on the turntable and the scrape of furniture being moved. Johnnie Ray's melodious voice would be singing a love song, laughter, my mother's voice, giggles, a man's groans, voices, and finally the door closing; the uncle's visit had ended.

The one thing those visits taught me were the words to the latest songs. Before I started school I didn't know who 'Jack and Jill' were and I hadn't felt fingers climbing my arm to the words of 'Itsy bitsy spider'; in fact, I didn't know one line from a nursery rhyme, but I could sing every verse of Johnnie Ray's 'Walking My Baby Back Home'.

When I finally left our room I entered one that reeked of cigarettes, cigars, beer and another fishy type of smell, which always lingered in the air after an uncle's visit. I didn't know what it was, just that my nose wrinkled with distaste as soon as I smelled it.

I have one vivid memory of my mother. It is of the last afternoon that I was home when an uncle visited and, after hearing the door shut, I had ventured into the sitting room. Gloria was lying on the settee showing a large expanse of white dimpled thigh above laddered stockings. Her eyes were shut and puffs of breath pushed themselves out of her lipstick-smeared mouth, along with a trickle of spit that was clinging to the corner of her lips. Her face, which had looked so pretty earlier with its powder-pale skin and red lips, now appeared flushed and flaccid as though the gin had soaked into her skin, loosening it from the framework of her bones.

In the ashtray was something that looked like a balloon that had lost its air. A pair of black lacy panties lay tossed on the floor. Her bottle of gin was almost empty so I knew two things: left alone she would sleep for some time, but if forced awake her temper would explode.

Looking at her, I hoped my baby sister Denise wouldn't waken, for if her wails and cries penetrated Gloria's slumbers then our bedroom would become my only retreat. I had learnt that Gloria's hand would lash out when she was annoyed, and I got the brunt of it when John was at school.

But my sister never seemed to wake on the days the uncles called. John told me later it was because of the medicine Gloria gave her.

Chapter Two

We three boys slept in one room. Davie slept on a small put-u-up while John and I shared an old stained mattress on an ill-fitting double-bed base.

John, who was old enough to feel apprehension at both Gloria's unpredictable behaviour and the uncle's visits, showed little of his feelings in the daytime. However, during the night when sleep gave his fears free rein, those worries plagued him. It was then that his bladder often opened, while he tossed and turned restlessly in his sleep, and I would wake to a wet bed.

I knew he was ashamed of wetting the bed so I would try and help him hide the damp sheets from Gloria. Her method of dealing with the problem was a hard blow to the head and a torrent of abuse.

'You dirty little bleeder,' she screamed the first time it happened, a grimace of disgust distorting her thickly lipsticked mouth. 'Well, you can sleep in it. I'm not wasting soap on your filth.' And with that she stomped into the second bedroom where our baby sister, disturbed by the loud sounds of aggression, was howling.

John's face flushed both from the pain of the blow and the look of contempt on his mother's face, for Gloria's approval was something he constantly sought. I had John to take care of me, Davie had both of us, but John had no one and, although I was too young then to understand this, I touched his arm in an attempt to comfort and reassure him.

Davie would do what he always did when there was shouting: bite his bottom lip, swallow back his tears, stretch out his hand and place it trustingly in mine.

When John was at school my little brother followed me around like a cute little puppy. I was the one he looked up to and I in turn looked up at John; whatever happened, he was my hero.

It was John who, last thing at night, stood guard for me at the outside privy. Gloria would just tell me to take myself down those stairs. She insisted I was old enough to go on my own and should stop making a fuss. But John would look up from whatever he was doing and give me a reassuring look.

'Come on, Robbie,' he would say. 'I'll come with you, I need to go myself.'

Without being told, John knew that I was frightened, almost in equal parts, of the dark and of Mrs Stone, the landlady. She was the owner of the three-storeyed house that was home to four families. Her flat was on the ground floor and from behind her door and the twitching net curtains of the front-room windows she monitored all the comings and goings in that house. Every time we needed access to the back-yard toilet we knew what awaited us, so we delayed as long as possible. Finally there was no alternative; we needed to 'go'.

However hard we tried to creep silently down the uncarpeted, creaky flight of stairs, she seemed to have a sixth sense that told her small boys were approaching. She would fling open her door and give us a hard stare as she looked for some misdemeanour she could blame us for. She was a small woman with a pale face and mousy hair caught up in a tight bun, who would not have caught my attention had I seen her on the street. But when I met her in the house there was something about her ramrod-straight figure, her stern, cold look and her harsh words accompanied by a clip round the ear that made me quake with fear.

She'd often be standing on the doorstep and I had to wriggle past her body, which, small as it was, appeared large enough to fill the doorway.

'This is a respectable place,' was her favourite mantra, one that seemed to deny all knowledge of Gloria's activities.

'Wipe your feet, boys,' she said every time, a command that was usually followed by another of her favourite chants: 'Walk, don't run.'

'Hope you don't grow up to be like your brothers,' she would say to little Davie. Knowing his 'still a baby' status kept him safe, he just screwed up his eyes and ignored her.

A cuff round the head was delivered to whoever was nearest and then, with another snort of disapproval, she would stomp up the few steps leading into the dark hall and disappear behind her front door.

Her departure always left John and me grinning sheepishly at each other. 'Silly old biddy,' he would say bravely and I would instantly relax, giggle and nod my head in loyal agreement.

Then John would flash that special smile of his, the one that was just for me. I can see it now, sort of conspiratorial, as if to say, 'It's just you and me, brother, just us two against the adult world.'

Once a week, without fail, Mrs Stone climbed the stairs to our top-floor rooms to confront our mother about our bad behaviour.

'Those hooligans of yours have …' – and the list of complaints about our misdeeds would follow.

We had left the outside toilet dirty.

We had wasted the squares of cut-up newspaper that passed for toilet paper.

We had left the lights on.

We had made too much noise on the stairs.

We had cheeked her.

No accusation went without further comments inferring that it was all Gloria's fault. She didn't discipline us enough and we ran wild.

Our mother, who feared losing the rooms, never pointed out that three boys going up and down uncarpeted stairs were bound to make some noise. As well as the trips to the outside lavatory, we were often struggling to carry Davie's pushchair or were weighed down by bags of shopping as we trudged up to the top floor. Of course there were times when we forgot to be quiet, normally when we were excited and racing out to play or had been given a few pennies to go and buy sweets.

Instead of defending us against the barrage of accusations, Gloria smacked John and me around the head. 'Say you're sorry. Do you hear me?' she would command, in a voice that we knew was pointless to argue with.

'You don't know how lucky you are having a nice home like this,' she continued, more to appease the accuser than for our benefit. Looking down at our scuffed shoes, we shuffled our feet and made our apologies to Mrs Stone, which were received with a dismissive sniff and followed with a final comment of 'Don't let it happen again.' After that she left, stomping loudly down the stairs. It was hard not to get the giggles as we were convinced that she made more noise than we ever did.

No sooner did Mrs Stone's footsteps fade than Gloria turned on us again.

'Showing me up, that's what you do,' she screamed. 'It's you that brings that old biddy up the stairs.' And an angry slap would follow, aimed at whoever was closest.

But on Sunday mornings Gloria was almost friendly to us. For on Sundays all the other occupants of Devonshire Place, including Mrs Stone, went to church. This meant that for a couple of hours we had the washroom to ourselves.

Before John did his chores he would fill the tin bath for Gloria using brownish hot water, which came from a rusty old boiler. With a cigarette in the corner of her mouth, a glass of gin in her hand and the latest *True Romance* magazine under her arm, she took herself down the three flights of stairs for an hour of privacy and leisurely ablutions.

Once she returned to her bedroom she started covering her body with powder and lotions, shouting to us that it was our turn to bath. John and I quickly stripped our bed of the foul urine-smelling sheets, gathered up Davie's too and then down we would all go. The tin bath was emptied and refilled and John, being the eldest, jumped in first then Davie and I bathed together.

After the three of us had washed and scrubbed ourselves clean it was the sheets' turn. They were dumped in the now-scummy soapy water, rubbed and squeezed by all of us then hoisted onto the line to dry. Another set, clean but equally as grey, would then be put onto our beds.

Doing our washing on a Sunday gave the rest of the tenants and Mrs Stone another reason to complain, but on those occasions Gloria stood her ground, making us almost look like a united family unit.

'John's at school all week,' was her excuse, 'and Robbie's too young to manage on his own. It's their bedding, so they must clean it. Don't want them growing up expecting women to do all the work, do you?'

And on another occasion, following the landlady's particularly bad-tempered list of our misdeeds, her parting shot was: 'Anyhow you keep telling me they're dirty and smelly. Well, they're not now.'

A few months earlier when our baby sister arrived, John and I were filled with curiosity.

Silently we crept into Gloria's bedroom. We never thought of it as being a room that belonged to two people, for with its mess of discarded clothes, pots of cream and underwear hanging over a chair, she had marked it as her territory. There was virtually no evidence of Stanley's presence in that room at all; just a single drawer for his underclothes and socks and a hanger, pushed to the back of the wardrobe, that held his spare pair of trousers, one jacket and a couple of shirts. In fact, except for a dish containing his shaving brush and razor, there were no personal possessions to show Stanley's existence anywhere in the flat.

We hovered around the small chest of drawers where our sister slept on a nest of old towels in a wedged-open drawer. Gazing down at her, we felt there was something about her tiny scrunched-up face, that fuzz of dark hair, those perfect little hands and the utter helplessness of her that made us want to pick her up and hold her.

Not daring to be responsible for waking her, we contented ourselves instead with reaching out our hands to touch her. John stroked the top of her head gently and I ran my finger against the silk of her cheek. Her eyelids flickered slightly and I watched with an awaking wonder the slight rise and fall of her tiny chest and listened to her faint breath. I didn't have the words in my head to describe how she made me feel. I was still only four and a half when she was born but I just knew I liked looking at her. And I liked the word 'sister'.

'Leave her alone!' my mother shouted whenever she saw us creeping towards her room. 'You think I want her awake? I've got enough to do with you lot.' Her scarlet-tipped hand clutching its ever-present cigarette flapped in our direction as she shooed us away.

'Go outside, will you? And take Davie with you. Bleeding brats, always under my feet. Give me some peace, why don't you?'

Faced with one of Gloria's unpredictable moods, when she needed no provocation to lash out with her hands and tongue, we would quickly leave the house.

John and I knew that after an hour it would be safe to return. By then she would have consoled herself with enough gin to be, if not reasonably amiable, then asleep or near enough to unconsciousness to ignore us completely.

At that age I was unaware that my mother, with the smell of gin and cigarettes on her breath and cheap perfume on her body, was different from other mothers. I didn't know it was unusual for a woman to leave much of the homemaking and childcare to her eight-year-old son. Nor did I understand that other children had frequent baths, wore clean clothes most probably made by their mothers and ate regular home-cooked meals. In fact, I had very little idea of what a mother's role was meant to be. It was only when we went to the beach or the park and saw mothers hug and kiss their children, holding their hands to keep them safe and drying their tears when they cried, that we got an inkling of a different sort of mothering.

'Sissies!' John and his mates would say to each other as they placed their hands on their hips, stuck out their elbows and swaggered past those scenes with little boys' bravado.

But in a curious way it was Gloria's indifference to our well-being that gave us the freedom to have that special last summer together; that summer where we played, swam in the sea and laughed with such joyous abandon, unaware that we only had a few months left before our lives changed forever. It was during those golden days that the bonds already formed between us boys grew and strengthened. And over the years when we were separated and silently called out to each other it was the power of those bonds that kept our three spirits connected and enabled us to survive.

Chapter Three

Before John's school holiday started I especially liked Saturdays. John was home all day and the nicest of the uncles, a small, nervous-looking, ginger-haired man wearing grease-stained overalls and an embarrassed smile, would arrive for his weekly visit. He owned a small garage in town, one that repaired motorcars as well as selling petrol.

John had discovered that Saturday was the day this particular uncle's wife went shopping and met up with her friends for afternoon tea at one of St Helier's recently opened cafés. We learnt that it was worth us delaying our departure, for this uncle handed out generous incentives to encourage us to leave and stay out of the way for some time.

'Hello, boys,' was his standard greeting as, with a crooked smile on his face and eyes cast down to avoid our collective stare, his hand quickly delved into his deep overall pocket and reappeared seconds later holding two shiny half crowns.

'You don't want to be staying indoors on a nice day like this. Here – take this money and buy yourself ice-creams.'

'Thank you, sir,' John and I would say in unison before turning and leaving. Barely suppressing our glee we would take Davie's hand and pull him along as we clattered down the stairs. The lure of unlimited ice-cream or sweets was stronger than our fear of Mrs Stone. Davie was willing to walk, taking the biggest steps he could to keep pace with us bigger boys, but on those days our usual patience was stretched as we were in too much of a hurry to get to the shop nearest to the beach front. John would place him in the pram, then push it determinedly towards the shops as we planned what purchases we would make. Ice-creams, lemon sherbet, gobstoppers or the illicit chewing gum that Gloria so hated; five shillings would buy lots, John assured me confidently.

We settled on ice-cream as Davie would be able to eat this easily, although half of it always ran down his front and up his sleeve because he had still not learnt to catch the melting drips with his tongue. Once the cone was gone and the last of the sweet ice-cream had been licked off our hands, we made our way to either the park or the beach.

Most Saturdays we met up with John's gang of friends. They were boys whose parents never seemed to notice if they were home or not; boys who played marbles intent on winning, took over the swings, bounced energetically up and down on the seesaw, had scabbed knees, grimy fingernails and wore torn jumpers; boys whose childhood had disappeared long before the onset of puberty, boys who were miniature men, boys from the same type of families as us.

'Playing nanny, John?' the group called mockingly when they saw all three of us approaching.

'Shut your mouths!' was his response, but his wide grin showed there was no ill feeling. And they in turn laughed, a friendly chuckling laughter that showed they were really only joking.

There was something about my elder brother even then – a confidence in his stance, an impression of not caring what other people thought – that made the boys understand that beneath that good humour was a temper. It was a temper that might be slow to rise but one they would be safer not waking, so the teasing always dried up almost before it began.

Packets of cigarettes and boxes of matches would appear. Cupping their hands to protect the flame from the wind, the boys formed a circle – one from which I was excluded.

'You're too young,' said John sternly to me when I tried putting my hand out for a puff of the shared cigarette. I would watch the smoke rising up, see the cigarette being passed around the circle of conspirators until there was nothing left and wonder silently when I would be old enough to join their group.

As we headed for the play area we would see neatly dressed children being pushed on the swings by their mothers. The colourful ribbons in the girls' plaited hair streamed out behind them and the little boys' ties flew over their shoulders. As our group approached, the mothers would stop the swings, order the children off and, with a glare of disapproval in our direction, would take their children's hands and move off to the slide or the roundabouts.

All the swings were then commandeered by us boys. Davie would be begging to join us but John always took him a few feet away to the baby section where there were small boxy swings with a metal safety bar in front. Checking that he was firmly seated and secure, John would give him a few firm pushes to get him started before running over to join his mates. Last year I too had been placed on the baby swings, but that summer John allowed me to swing on the same ones as him and his friends, not only sitting on the wooden seat but standing on it just like them. 'Hold fast now, Robbie,' he would remind me.

I swung so high I thought I would go over the bar. I clutched the metal chains so tightly that the knuckles on both hands were white. I pushed my body backwards and forwards and pumped my legs as hard as I could. In and out they went, higher and higher I flew, until the chains buckled, stopping me from going right over the metal bar. I bent my body as far back as possible until my feet and head were almost in a straight line, looked at the blue sky, felt the wind rush by me and laughed out loud at the sheer exhilarating freedom of it. And those bigger boys laughed, first at my determined efforts at keeping up with them and then with me as they felt the same thrill that I did.

'Tell whose brother he is,' they said, patting me on the back, and I, feeling their approval, glowed with pride.

Go-carts appeared in the park, made out of orange boxes and the bases of old prams that had been found discarded on rubbish dumps. Rope was tied to them and Davie and I were placed inside. John and his friends ran round and round the park pulling those carts while Davie and I screamed out our enjoyment. The park-keeper tried to chase us away but we always found another area out of his sight.

'Hey, Robbie! Do you fancy an apple?' John asked me on one of those days.

A picture of a juicy red apple floated in front of my eyes and I nodded my head with enthusiasm.

'We got enough money left?' I asked. I was still too young to work out what change we should have.

John gave a little laugh. 'Don't cost. You'll see. Just take Davie's pram and watch. Give us a few minutes then follow. Got it?'

I put my hands over the pram's handle and watched John running up the road, his arms swinging and his head down. He slowed to a brisk trot in front of the greengrocers, shot his hand out, and an apple disappeared into his pocket.

I felt my eyes grow big just seeing him do that. I waited as he had told me then followed him slowly.

He had only had time to steal one apple so we all had to share it.

It tasted very good.

On another occasion he told me he had to stop to get something from one of the local shops. A tin of corned beef for our tea, he told me.

The shopkeeper viewed our trio with something I recognised as suspicion until John took one of our half crowns out of his pocket and placed it on the counter. He gave his order and then, looking up at the top shelf, he pretended to see something else he wanted. It didn't matter what it was because he had no intention of buying it.

'I'll have that as well,' he would tell the shopkeeper. 'My Ma said for me to buy it.' The shopkeeper had to stand on a set of steps to reach it and, once his back was turned, quick as a flash John's hands reached out to pick up several bars of chocolate. He gave me a wink as he hastily slid them into his pocket.

When the shopkeeper put the object on the counter he would just say he had made a mistake and paid for the tin of corned beef or whatever it was that Gloria had asked him to bring home with us. I felt a surge of pride at my older brother's antics.

Once out of the shopkeeper's view he broke up one of the bars into equal amounts for him and me and a smaller piece for Davie. They tasted even better than the apple. Before we reached Devonshire Place we stopped to spit on a ragged handkerchief so that we could wipe our faces. We didn't want telltale rings of chocolate around our mouths giving us away to Mrs Stone or Gloria.

'Now keep your mouths shut when we get in,' John instructed Davie and me.

I nodded my head vehemently in agreement even though we both knew that the chances were that Gloria would be in a gin-induced stupor when we returned. And even on the rare occasions when she had run out of alcohol, she showed little interest in where we had been. So long as we weren't under her feet, she didn't give a damn.

Chapter Four

John had been taught to swim by some older boys, and that summer he decided to teach both Davie and me — not in the sea but in what was left of a huge man-made tidal pool on the beach. It was the remains of a horseshoe-shaped swimming pool that the Germans had built during their occupation of Jersey in the war. When the tide came in it filled up and the water in it remained calm whatever was happening out at sea. John said it was safer for swimming lessons than the sea and he produced the rubber inner tubes of old car tyres cadged from my mother's Saturday uncle.

'How did you get them?' I asked.

'Told him I needed them to teach you two to swim. Said Saturday was the best day. That did it,' he said with a grin. 'Silly codger couldn't wait to help out if it meant we would be out of the house when he comes round. Told me he would still give me those half crowns and all, but not to come to his garage in the daytime again. Can go round Friday night when he's locking up. He was nearly shitting himself in case his wife saw me there.' John laughed at the memory. And I, not really understanding his meaning, grinned back at him anyhow.

John threw me an old tattered pair of shorts that he had long ago grown out of. I donned them, then we helped Davie off with his clothes and into an old pair of pants.

The orange inner tubes went round our bodies twice. Once John was satisfied they were firmly secured he raced us across the sand for our first swimming lesson. That day we gambolled in the pool, splashing, kicking, laughing, swallowing water, spluttering and laughing again. After a week our shoulders had turned pink and our noses were peeling, but we could stay afloat without help. By the end of the summer we had all turned a dark golden brown. John's thick blond hair was bleached nearly white and Davie and I were proudly swimming without the aid of those orange tubes.

We found a discarded bucket left on the beach by a visiting tourist and purloined it with glee. When we were not in the water Davie and I used it to scoop up sand and build sandcastles. John considered that activity was strictly for babies and preferred us all to play the games he made up. 'Castaways' was the most popular. Influenced by the story of *Treasure Island,* which John had listened to at school, it involved answering to different names, searching the rock pools and beach for food and driftwood, and lighting a bonfire with a box of forbidden matches.

'I'm Long John Silver and you, Robbie, are Boy Friday,' John informed me.

'Who's me?' Davie asked.

'The bloody parrot!' John shouted, laughing, but then, seeing Davie's face drop at being teased, he quickly ruffled his hair to show it was only a joke.

As castaways we wanted to be on the beach the whole time. We would have built a shelter and lived there if we could. As soon as we woke we tried to make our escape from Gloria. Unless she had chores lined up for John, such as running to the shops for cigarettes or lemonade, she mostly looked relieved at having a peaceful day in front of her.

But even she demanded that we ate some kind of breakfast before we left.

'Hey, John!' she yelled through the bedroom door in what might have passed for maternal concern. 'Get you and your brothers something to eat before you go out. And make a brew for me while you're at it. You can bring it in here. I've got to get more sleep; I'm bleeding tired.'

John dutifully put the kettle on, poured cornflakes into three bowls and sniffed the milk bottle to check if the contents were sour before pouring it into the bowls and sprinkling them with heaped spoons of sugar. He cut the loaf of bread into thick slices, spread it with butter and strawberry jam and poured milk into plastic mugs for Davie and me, then made enough tea to have a cup himself after taking one in to Gloria. Davie and I gobbled our food down and, once the last bite had been swallowed, clothes were hastily pulled on and our hands and faces wiped on a shared facecloth. We saw no need for more than that; after all, we were going into the sea.

'Bye,' we called out to Gloria. Sometimes, if she was in a good mood, she would call out, 'Hey, John, pass me my purse. Suppose you lot better get some chips to eat later on.' She would give us the money carefully counted out. Sometimes if she was feeling generous there was enough for a fruit juice or lemonade as well. John always said that was so we didn't need to return home to eat lunch, and I realise now that was true. When the money was pocketed and the word 'thanks' muttered, she had a few last words to say, which seldom varied: 'Don't want that old biddy bothering me, so you mind you're quiet on the bleeding stairs,' she would shout after us before she flopped back onto her makeup-stained pillows.

We assumed whenever we thought of her that baby Denise had been fed earlier. The tin of Cow & Gate formula milk was open on the kitchen table amidst the debris of dirty feeding bottles, dummies and overflowing ashtrays. Sometimes we heard her cry in the night, but usually when we left the house she was asleep. I suppose Gloria must have been taking care of her somehow when we weren't around.

Once out of the house we ran down the road as fast as we could. We wanted to reach the beach before local families and holidaymakers carrying deckchairs, baskets of food and protective floppy sun hats put in an appearance. When the beach was empty we could pretend that it was ours alone.

Once there, the first thing we did was to jump into the pool. Afterwards we lay on the warm sand and let the sun's rays dry us off. John would go and buy us lemonade – he always had some money left from the last visit of the Saturday uncle if Gloria hadn't given us anything that morning – and then it was time to play the game.

'Castaways,' John told me, 'have to be able to find their own food.' All we needed, he assured us, was a packet of salt, an old baby's bottle with its teat intact and a bucket.

'Come on, Robbie,' he said impatiently. 'I'm going to show you what real castaways do.' Picking up my clothes and the bucket I followed him, with Davie bringing up the rear, to where he told me there were plenty of razor fish to catch. Then he informed me that not only was there food under the sand but winkles could also be found between the rocks. We could get those later, once the beach became busier.

First I was given the task of filling the baby's bottle with water and stirring in lots of salt until it had dissolved. When that was done John showed me how easy it was to catch the razor fish.

'See those little bumps with holes in the top?' he said, pointing to a strip of beach that was pitted with tiny bumps. 'Them little bleeders are in there. See?' He took the bottle, squeezed the teat and aimed the mixture on to the tiny hole.

'Here it comes,' he said – and sure enough, something that looked a bit like Stanley's cut-throat razor was poking out of the sand.

'Now we have a little tug of war,' he said grinning. 'You do it, but pull gently mind or you'll just end up with its bleeding shell.'

I placed my hand tentatively on it, did as John instructed and pulled gently. There was a feeling of suction as it resisted me and then with a sudden plop it was in my hand. I had done it! I felt a grin split my face almost in two as I looked at my brother with astonished delight.

'It's easy!' I said nonchalantly.

'Good. You can fill the bucket up then.' John turned to saunter over to his friends, who had appeared on the beach.

'Hey, Robbie!' they yelled. 'Make sure you get enough for us and all, will ya?'

With their challenge ringing in my ears I made sure I got the hang of catching those fish that first afternoon. Flushed with success, I squirted that salty water down every hole I could see. Crouched on my haunches with the sand trickling warmly between my toes and the sun beating down on my neck and back, I waited impatiently for them to appear, which they always did after a few seconds. Davie squatted beside me, his mouth forming an 'oh' every time he saw the tip of the razor fish appear. He would squeal with delight when I successfully dropped one into the bucket. Deep in concentration, my tongue resting on my lower lip, I squirted and pulled until the old bucket that John had filled with fresh seawater was overflowing with the browny-grey shells of my catch.

'That keeps them alive until we are ready to eat them,' John had explained when he put the bucket next to me.

Later we looked in the crevices between the rocks for winkles. Even Davie helped pull them out and put them in our makeshift cooking pot – an old tin filled with water.

As Boy Friday, my tasks were extended to collecting firewood and I enlisted Davie as my helper. Anything that would burn we picked up. Bits of paper, twigs and pieces of driftwood were collected and placed in a pile in the quietest spot we could find. Then John made the bonfire; it was always him who was in charge of the matches.

When we got bored with the beach we wandered down to the port to look at the boats that were moored there. In the fifties it was mainly fishing boats and, of course, the ferries that went to English and French ports. The big, rugged, sunburnt fishermen worked on deck or sat on the quay mending their nets. To pass the time they would watch our trio. Maybe to them it seemed strange that we were out on our own with only an eight-year-old boy in charge. Whatever the reason for their interest, they were friendly and kind towards us. They showed us around the boats, bought us cakes and squash from the nearby café and, once satisfied that we had a home to return to that night, asked few searching questions of us.

When John explained our game of Castaways to them, good-natured, deep, male laughter erupted and they contributed a piece of newspaper filled with shrimps, the tiny ones that were too small to sell but tasted just right to us when we boiled them and added them to our Castaways meal. John always cooked this on the beach as far away from the other holidaymakers as possible. We rarely took anything home. Without putting it into words, we knew Gloria liked the rooms to herself and her male friends. That was why she was happy to give us money for chips. But we also knew that if she discovered how adept we had become at feeding ourselves, her limited generosity might have ceased.

After our meal was finished we walked home, pushing the pram with a sleepy Davie inside, staggered up the stairs and made our way to bed. There was rarely any sign of Gloria when we returned. Her bedroom door would be firmly closed.

All too soon the long, warm, sunny days grew cooler, twilight came earlier and one by one the last days of that summer slid seamlessly away. I wanted them to last for ever and ever, but they didn't.

I have sometimes asked myself whether it was wishes mixed with memory that created those perfect golden days in my mind. Did that combination heighten the warmth of the sun, paint butterfly wings brighter, make birdsong sweeter and laughter ring out more joyously?

And was it the sheer force of me wishing the last summer of my childhood to be perfect that lessened the force of Gloria's blows as she became more temperamental and unpredictable, camouflaged Stanley's deepening depression as he became virtually invisible in our lives, disguised Denise's constant cries and grizzles of hunger and distress, and made our stomachs fuller?

I don't know, because whenever I look back to that time, all these years later, I see it through a haze where even the dust motes were tinged with gold and every day was idyllic. I remember the women in bright cotton dresses, the blueness of the sky, the white horses that tipped the sea's azure waves, the tangerine sun and on those rare days when small puffs of cloud marbled the sky even the rain was perfumed with the scent of flowers.

But I also remember that once that summer ended an insidious feeling of disquiet entered our home; a warning I didn't hear that soon our lives were going to change forever.

Chapter Five

September arrived and I was due to start at the local
primary school, a subject that hadn't been broached by
Gloria right up until the day before I was due to enrol. For
once, she told us not to leave the house. Didn't John have
to sort his school things out? Didn't she have to find something for me to wear? Didn't she have enough to do as it
was? Hadn't the bleeding baby kept her awake all night?
We were not to go anywhere and that was that. After that
tirade she spent the entire morning rummaging through
cupboards pulling out cardboard boxes and muttering
words such as 'Where are the bastard things? Bleeding
brats. Ah! Here they are!' Then with a cigarette clutched
in one hand, a pile of clothes tucked under her arm and a
scowl on her flushed face, she marched into our room.

Her search had evidently been successful. She had
found some old school clothes of John's, ones that he had
outgrown, which she deposited in a crumpled heap on the
bed. A pair of black lace-up shoes was thrust at me. At her
instruction I tried them on and found that not only were
they very scuffed at the toe and heel but also that my feet
stepped right out of them.

'They're far too big!' I cried plaintively.

'Oh, just put two pairs of socks on and some newspaper in the toes,' mumbled Gloria in exasperation. She took a deep drag on her cigarette, blew smoke in the air and squinted at me through resentful, half-closed eyes.

'Money don't grow on trees, ya know, so don't think I'm going to waste it on buying stuff you'll grow out of before the year is out. These will do ya, and Davie too when he goes to bleeding school.'

'Hey, John,' she said turning her attention to him. 'Get some of Stanley's shoe polish out and give those shoes a good clean, seeing Robbie's so particular and all. Clean yours while you're at it. And sort that stuff out for yourselves, will ya? I can't do everything round here.' She pointed to the pile of tatty garments scattered on our bed.

One by one I picked up each piece of clothing and looked at it with something approaching dismay. At five years old I had not reached the age where clothes or style were important to me, but I was already nervous about starting school the next day and when I saw the sloppy grey jumper worn thin at the elbows, the frayed collars and cuffs of the shirts, the short trousers that due to John's tree climbing had a rip on one pocket, and a number of ill-matched long grey socks with holes in the heels or toes, I knew that I was not going to look the same as the other boys on their first day of school.

'Ah, come on, Robbie,' said John when he saw my downcast face. 'I'll get those shoes shiny for you. You'll look all right tomorrow.'

For the first time John's voice failed to console me; I
knew I wouldn't.

The next morning when we got ready for school,
Gloria was still in bed so we crept round our room as
silently as possible. Neither of us wanted to bump into her.
I dressed in what John and I thought were the best of the
clothes she had given me, hastily ate some cornflakes, and
gulped down a glass of milk, then, standing at the sink, I
wiped my face and hands with a damp cloth and damped
my hair down, copying John's early morning ablutions. I
was ready to leave for my first day at school. John grabbed
two apples, some cream crackers and a lump of cheddar
cheese from the pantry cupboard and stuffed them into a
pocket.

'That's our lunch,' he told me. 'They give us milk at
school. Come on, let's go.'

I felt a pang when I saw Davie's sad little face watching us silently from the bedroom door and gave him what
I hoped was a reassuring smile; he looked completely
desolate at our departure. His eyes filled with tears and his
lower lip trembled at the thought of being left all alone in
the flat – well, as good as, for Gloria was likely to sleep in
until lunchtime unless Denise's hungry wails woke her
sooner.

A wave of nausea overcame me as I followed John
down the stairs. In an attempt to reassure me he explained
how classes were made up of children all around the same
age so I already knew I would not be sitting with him. I
was bothered when I was told that I would be in a section

called the Infants whilst he was in the Juniors and wondered miserably just how far away from me he would be.

'Cheer up,' he said. 'They don't eat ya, ya know.' He gave my arm a brotherly pat. But I still fretted, wondering what the day ahead was going to bring.

The school was a sprawling, single-storey building, its entrance in one road and the exit in another parallel to it. As we approached I saw children of all ages were standing in groups in various parts of the large tar-covered playground. I heard a buzz of high-pitched conversation, shrieks of laughter and, over the general clamour, my brother's name being called.

'John, over here!' called one of the boys I recognised from the park.

'See ya in a sec, got to do something first,' John yelled back.

Suddenly I realised that he wanted to be with his own friends, not shepherding me, his little brother, about.

John walked with me to where a pretty young teacher was dealing with the new arrivals.

'Miss, this is Robbie, my brother,' he said by way of introduction.

And he left me there.

My heart sank.

The teacher told me her name was Miss Darby. She smiled and put her hand gently on my shoulder. I knew she was trying to be nice. I heard her ask me a question, something about what I liked doing, but all I wanted to do was run after my brother. Out of the corner of my eye I watched him saunter away.

Would he at least turn and give me that special smile?

He didn't. Instead, without a backward glance, he rushed up to a group of boys his own age who were gathered on the far side of the playground. They were boys I knew from the park and on the beach but instinctively I knew that it didn't matter how often those bigger boys had played with me during the holidays; they were not going to accept my inclusion to their group here within the school grounds.

I felt a swift pang of desolation, a sense of loss that increased when, looking around me, I realised that I was the only child there on his or her own. The Infants area was full of mothers delivering their small offspring. Mothers bent down lovingly and shoelaces were tied yet again, crisp white collars were straightened and ties were gently adjusted. I watched them kissing bandbox-clean children a quick reassuring goodbye, heard them say words like 'darling' and 'be good' and 'love' then saw them stop at the gates to turn and give one last final wave, wiping their eyes and digging for a handkerchief to blow their noses. A lump came into my throat as I remembered the times in the park when children such as these had held their mothers' hands or been pushed on the swings by a caring adult and for the first time in my life I think I had an inkling of what a mother really should be like.

The teacher clapped her hands and twenty pair of eyes turned to look at her. She told us to form a neat line and follow her into the classroom. We fell into line and, backs straight as brooms, we formally entered the education system.

She led the way into a light, airy room furnished with tiny wooden desks with low seats attached to them, each meant for two people. She told us to sit. There were hesitant movements as small children, some flushed with excitement, others tearful and woebegone, chose who they wanted to sit next to. Little girls in grey pinafore dresses or pleated skirts and blue jumpers sat next to other neat, clean little girls. Boys wearing blue blazers and short grey trousers sat next to freshly scrubbed ones who were their mirror image. Before the day was out best friends would be made – friendships that would perhaps endure for years to come. Little girls would hold hands and talk about their dolls and little boys would select 'boys' toys' from the box in the classroom and choose someone to play with them.

Nobody sat next to me.

Our names were called and our teacher looked down at a book in front of her and ticked when we answered 'Here, Miss,' as we had been instructed.

That first morning she gave us books with big letters of the alphabet and pictures. I recognised them. John had shown me letters when he had read to us from the comics. I also knew what one and one was. I had learnt that from running errands for Gloria and buying ice-cream. I already knew that shopkeepers were unhappy if I asked for more things than I had money for.

'Good, Robbie,' she said when I got my first question right.

I began to feel less nervous about being at school.

Later that morning, she produced a wooden clock painted in bright colours and decorated with small white ducks, which she stood on her desk. She placed the hands on a 3 and a 6 and asked if anyone knew what time that was. I knew. John had taught me, using the clock in the kitchen at home. It was so that I would know when he was due back from school.

'Very good, Robbie,' Miss Darby said with another smile.

I began to feel even better.

She passed out crayons and paper. 'Draw whatever you want,' she said when one little girl asked what she should do with them. My hours of drawing when I had to amuse Davie paid off. I drew a house and placed stick figures of a man and a woman next to it. Then I drew four smaller ones. And lastly with the dark brown crayon I made a large oval with a smaller one on top and lines representing legs and pointy ears.

'That's my family,' I told the teacher.

'And is that where you live?' she asked, but my silence told her it wasn't. She didn't ask if we had a dog.

'That's very good, Robbie,' she said instead.

I decided I might like school after all.

We had a break and gold-topped bottles of milk with straws in them were given to us. Then we were sent into the playground and that was when my burgeoning enjoyment of school abruptly ceased.

I had forgotten that I looked different from the other children. Nor had I had time to learn what could happen to a child that doesn't fit in. I just walked out into that playground and started heading towards the far end of it with only two thoughts in my head: the teacher had liked me and I wanted to tell John about my successful morning.

I felt the hands on my back before I had a chance to see who they belonged to. They gave me a push that sent me staggering and at the same time I heard a jeering voice.

'Stinky!' it said.

I tried to look round but I only saw a blur of faces. They seemed to be surrounding me. Then another boy, a couple of years older than me, pushed me hard in the chest. My arms flew out as I staggered backwards, trying to keep my balance.

'Yer Ma's a Jerry bag,' he hissed, 'and you're a stinky Kraut.'

What on earth did he mean? I hadn't heard those expressions before.

The first boy pushed me in the back again and suddenly there were pushes coming from both sides and I was staggering backwards and forwards with the sound of their mocking laughter ringing in my ears. I knew the laughter was not just from them for a crowd of boys had gathered and seemed to be egging them on.

I heard a shout in the distance, running feet, and then my brother's voice rang out.

'Leave him alone, you bleeding creeps!' he shouted.

I saw his arm go out and connect with one of my tormentors' heads and almost simultaneously he spun sideways and kicked out with his foot.

'Break it up now!' I heard a man's stern voice say and looking up I saw the flushed, angry face of the headmaster. He'd popped into our classroom that morning and Miss Darby had told us all who he was.

'Might have known it was you, Garner,' he said crossly, looking at John.

Then he looked at me and I noted the expression of distaste that flitted across his face.

'Oh, another one of your family. Robbie, isn't it? So now we'll have more trouble, I suppose.' He turned to the watching crowd. 'Get to your classrooms, boys. The bell has just gone. And you, little Robbie, just remember I'll be watching you. Your brother's nothing but trouble and it looks as though you're cut from the same cloth.'

He strode off, leaving John and me standing alone. One of his friends came over. 'Let's get that lot later,' he said, but John just shook his head. 'Ah, leave it.'

'John, what's a Jerry bag?' I asked.

'Shut up, Robbie,' he said and the anger in his voice shocked me into obedient silence. 'Go back to your bit of the playground. And stay there on your breaks. Stop looking for me all the time.' Offering me no comfort, he abruptly turned his back on me and joined his friends. Dragging my feet I unwillingly walked up to where my teacher was herding her charges together and followed them in.

The Infants broke up half an hour earlier than the Juniors but I hung around on the street outside waiting for my brother to come out. He looked irritated instead of pleased to see me when he came out of the school gates but within a few moments his good humour had returned.

'So how was it?' he asked, without any mention of the fight.

'All right,' I answered, but I refused to be put off asking the questions that had been spinning around my head all afternoon. 'John, what's a Jerry bag?' Gloria might not have been a good mother but she was the only one I knew and I had understood from the tone that that word wasn't just an ordinary insult but something very bad.

My brother sighed. 'Someone who likes Krauts,' he said at last.

'What's a Kraut?'

'A German soldier. A bleeding Hun, that's what.'

I went quiet then, for even at five I had heard the stories of the German occupation of Jersey during the war and I knew that they had been our enemy.

I had never heard of anyone being friends with one.

'That's why she hates going out,' John blurted before turning to me. 'Stanley's your dad, Robbie, and mine – mine was an American.' His pale grey eyes looked into mine as though daring me to contradict him.

But how could I when I didn't know what he meant?

Chapter Six

'The headmaster wants to see you,' my teacher told me several weeks after I had started school. 'This lady,' and she indicated a plump, middle-aged woman who had just come into the classroom, 'is going to take you to him.'

I shot her a scared look. I had been told that the headmaster only asked to see us when we had done something very bad and that a punishment would always follow.

'Don't worry, Robbie,' she said with a reassuring smile. 'He just wants to give you and your brother something.'

As I followed the lady along the long corridor I hoped she was right. My mind scurried round trying to think of any misdeeds, but none came to me. On the other hand I couldn't think of anything the headmaster could be going to give me.

The lady smiled at me again when she knocked on a large wooden door.

'Don't look so worried, Robbie. You've not done anything wrong,' she whispered just before he shouted out 'Come in!' and she opened the door.

To my surprise John was standing there.

For a moment I felt a wave of panic. Had something bad happened at home? I looked at John but he avoided my gaze and stared at the floor instead. That added to my panic.

I held my breath and waited.

'Robbie,' the headmaster said, 'I've spoken to your brother about the way you both come to school. We have written to your mother on several occasions and someone from the welfare has called on her.'

The words floated in the air above me. I tried to catch them and hold them still so that I could understand what they meant but before I could do that more followed, such as 'unacceptable', 'filthy', 'smelly', 'offensive' and 'can no longer be tolerated', before he paused for breath.

I knew he was waiting for me to speak but I couldn't think of anything to say. What did he want us to do? Again I glanced at my brother hoping for some help but I quickly saw there was to be none from that direction; he still appeared to find the floor more interesting than my presence for his gaze was firmly directed at it.

Seeing my confusion, the lady took pity on me and knelt down until she was at my height. She gently held my elbows, her brown eyes looked earnestly into mine as she explained, using words I could understand, the meaning of what the headmaster had been saying.

'What your headmaster is trying to tell you is that you must look better when you come to school. Your clothes are nearly worn away. And I know you are only a little boy so it's not your fault, but they smell as well. You've got to be clean and neat when you come here.' She paused for breath and I looked at her uncomprehendingly. After all, what could I do?

The headmaster started again. 'We have a charitable fund at our disposal for boys in your position and we have decided that you certainly qualify for a sum of money to be spent on you. Mrs Johnston,' he told us, indicating the lady who had brought me to his office, 'is going to take you shopping. She will choose the right clothes for you. In turn you two boys are to come to school with clean hair, hands and face. There is no excuse for you to come here dirty.' His hand snaked out and caught John's ear and he quickly inspected it. He continued: 'That means neck and ears, my boy. Yours are grey.'

I continued to stare at him; suddenly I didn't want to meet John's eyes. I had seen the blush that suffused his face until even the tips of his ears had turned a bright crimson. I knew he felt diminished somehow by the head-master's words and it was even worse that I, his little brother who hero-worshipped him, had been present to witness his embarrassment. I wondered if we could go – but no, the headmaster hadn't finished with us yet.

'One more thing. It's been reported to me that you never bring a lunch box with you. Is that right?'

'Yes, sir,' answered John, shuffling his feet and still inspecting the floor.

'Look at me when I'm talking to you,' the headmaster barked. John's head shot up. I saw his hands clench and knew that he wanted to be anywhere but in this room.

'Mrs Johnston will organise a charity lunch box for each of you,' he said dismissively.

I wanted to shout at that headmaster and tell him all about my wonderful brother. He had no idea who John really was. He had never seen how he cared for Davie and me and kept our flat as clean as he could. He didn't hear the abuse that Gloria heaped on him or see him run errands for his drunken mother who for some reason – maybe just because he was the eldest – seemed to blame him for the many misfortunes in her life. He just saw two uncared for and unloved children standing in front of him and judged them as being worthless. He gave no consideration to our pride because we were only two grubby boys who qualified for a charity hand-out. And once his duty was done, he dismissed us.

Mrs Johnston took us to a shop that stocked suitable school clothes for us. After she had chosen the most inexpensive but serviceable shirt, shoes, trousers and a jumper each, it was all wrapped into two parcels for us to take home.

On the way home, we were excited at receiving new clothes that would mean we fitted in better at school, but apprehensive about Gloria's possible reaction.

She screeched when John said he was getting the bath out. 'Where do you think the money's coming from to put in the gas meter?' John didn't answer. He just went to the jar where loose change was kept and took the money out.

And for the first time she backed down – not without muttering that no one was going to tell her how to bring up her kids, but the heart had gone out of her complaints.

'Oh, do what you want – you always do,' she finally said after John repeated that we had to be clean before we wore the new clothes.

The next day we were scrubbed clean. Dressed in our new uniforms and smelling of soap, we both, in different parts of the school, received a charity lunch box of food.

I felt the heat rise on the back of my neck when I was given mine. I just knew that every child in the class knew what that little container, placed carefully on my desk, meant. I could feel everyone looking at me as I opened it and examined the contents: hard-boiled egg sandwiches wrapped in greaseproof paper, a bottle of orange squash and a small piece of fruit cake. I would rather have had an apple and a piece of cheese from John's pocket – anything rather than the shame of a charity lunch box that marked us out as 'different' and 'unloved' just as clearly as our old, ragged clothes had done before.

Chapter Seven

A few weeks after we had been called to the headmaster's office, school broke up for the Christmas holidays. The festive season was cold and rainy that year – not that it made any difference to us.

We knew there wouldn't be a Christmas tree covered with imitation snow and draped with paper chains with a glittering star on top. Neither, we were sure, would there be a sack of presents waiting to surprise us. And there was no point looking for stockings stuffed with oranges and sweets at the foot of our beds.

We knew that other families celebrated with presents and special meals. We had seen brightly decorated rooms and trees with piles of presents sitting under their branches through the windows of other people's houses. And we could imagine how Christmas day would be in their homes: carpets strewn with wrapping paper torn off presents by excited small children, air perfumed with the rich smells of a mother's baking and dishes full of fruit, nuts and chocolates on the dining-room table.

If, when we saw those children who glowed with the confidence of being cared for, we felt emptiness, a hollow space under our ribs that should have been filled with love, we said nothing. For what is put into words becomes reality and we were happy, weren't we?

All the word Christmas meant to John and me was a day off school, and to Davie it meant even less. So that year when we woke on Christmas morning we were prepared to find it was just another day.

Our mouths fell open when we went into the sitting room and saw four parcels wrapped in brown paper and tied with string. Three smaller ones had been put on the table and a bigger one lay on the floor. John jabbed me in the ribs and we stared at each other. Davie ran over and grabbed one.

'Better leave that alone,' John said quickly.

'Where do they come from?' I asked.

'Not Father Christmas, that's for sure,' said John with a knowing laugh.

At that moment Gloria's door opened and Stanley came out with a huge grin on his face.

'Merry Christmas, boys,' he said. Then he called over his shoulder, 'Come on, Gloria. It's time to open our Christmas presents.'

Gloria, still in her old, stained dressing gown, with the baby on her hip and a cigarette in the other hand, stopped dead when she saw the parcels on the table.

'Bloody hell, what's this then?'

'You won't know until you've opened them,' Stanley answered. 'You all sit down and I'll hand them out.'

We three boys dived obediently onto the sagging couch. Gloria sank into her corner of it, one thinly plucked eyebrow raised enquiringly.

Stanley picked up a parcel and read out what he had written in pencil on the brown paper: 'To my dearest Gloria. Happy Christmas. Love, Stanley.'

'I hope you don't think I got you anything,' she said, snatching the present from him.

We watched her tear off the paper and give a squeal of surprise. Stanley had bought her the latest record by Johnnie Ray, 'Somebody Stole My Girl'. Gloria had been going on about it ever since its release.

'Do you like it then?' asked Stanley.

'Of course I do.' Gloria gave him a quick peck on the cheek. It was the first time I'd seen her show Stanley any affection and he flushed with pleasure.

Next it was Davie's turn. He was so excited he couldn't sit still. This was the first present anyone had ever given Davie in his life. His big blue eyes were shining as John helped him untie the string. He pulled out a small wooden toy soldier with a rifle over its shoulder.

Davie immediately dropped to the floor and began marching his soldier up and down.

'Here's yours, John,' said Stanley.

It was a wooden pencil box with a sliding lid.

'Thanks very much, Stanley,' said John politely but without much enthusiasm. 'That's just what I need for school.'

He gave Denise a soft little teddy bear and she shoved it straight into her mouth.

'And now it's your turn, Robbie.'

There was only one present left – the big one that lay on the floor. Stanley gave me a smile as I ran across to get it. My heart was pounding as if it was going to jump right out of my chest. I fumbled at the knot and ripped off the paper, then I gasped. It was a wooden easel, just the right size for me, and with it came a thick stack of drawing paper.

Stanley set it up for me.

'I know you like drawing, Robbie, so I thought now was the time for you to have this.'

I was flooded with such happiness I could hardly tear my eyes away from it.

John said, 'That's nice, Robbie,' but I could see something sad in his expression.

I rushed over to Stanley and hugged him around his legs and he gave me a pat on the head.

Maybe it was the excitement of the Christmas presents or maybe it was the gin but Stanley somehow persuaded Gloria to cook us lunch. Of course, she complained a bit but she ended up frying some pork bangers on the two-plate cooker. She also managed to make some lumpy mash and opened a tin of baked beans.

Stanley produced a punnet of jellied eels, which we had first, and a tin of peaches from South Africa was emptied into a bowl for afters. He'd also brought a bottle of sweet sherry and he poured some into a glass and gave each of us boys a taste. Davie took a sip and pulled such a funny face we all laughed. The only ones who didn't have any were Denise, who had wakened and was sitting propped up on the couch watching us all with interest, and Gloria.

'I'll stick to my own poison, thank you very much,' she said, holding out her glass for Stanley to top up with gin.

Although to other people that might not seem much of a Christmas lunch, it's one of my great memories of happiness. I can see us all now: Gloria with her head thrown back laughing, Stanley looking content, Davie excited, John relaxed, and me – I just wanted to get to my easel.

After we had eaten, Gloria put her new record on the turntable. The smooth tones of Johnnie Ray filled the room and Stanley got up and, with a mock bow, asked her to dance.

'Oh, go on with you,' she said. But she eventually agreed. She and Stanley started to dance and John picked up the baby. Holding her in his arms he slowly danced around the room with her. For once, Gloria didn't yell at him to leave her alone. I took Davie's hands and we did a sort of gallop around the room. We were all laughing and Davie started to shriek with delight.

'You lot had better keep it down or you'll have the old bitch from downstairs coming to complain,' was all Gloria said.

When the record was finished Gloria played it a couple more times before Stanley said the lunch and sherry had made him feel sleepy so he and Gloria went into her room and closed the door.

John walked over to the window and stared down at the street. It had started to rain earlier and was pelting down.

'Bleedin' rain,' he said. 'I wish it would stop so I could go and see my mates.'

But going out was the last thing I had in mind. I took a sheet of paper and carefully set it up on the easel. I fetched my crayons and started to draw a picture of us all dancing.

John found himself an old *Beano* to read and Davie and Denise fell fast asleep clutching their new toys but I was in another world as I worked on my picture. I let my imagination go and had us dancing around a Christmas tree. We were all smiling.

Later, when Gloria and Stanley came out of the bedroom, he turned on the radio so we could hear the Queen's speech. We'd missed the afternoon one but it was being repeated that evening. It didn't mean anything to us but we sat and listened quietly even though John made me giggle by looking at me cross-eyed. That earned me a sharp look from Gloria. She loved the royals and read every article about them in her magazines.

When the speech ended Stanley turned off the radio and Gloria held out her glass to him.

'Pour us another one,' she said. 'And this time take it easy on the lemonade.'

'Don't you think you should call it a day, Gloria?' said Stanley and as he said it I got an uneasy feeling in my stomach, knowing how suddenly Gloria's good humour could vanish.

'Don't you tell me what to do, you miserable git,' she slurred as she pulled herself off the couch. 'I'll get my own bleedin' drink. What do I need you for? Just because you gave me a stupid record you think you can tell me what to do. Why don't you just bugger off?'

I remember feeling sorry for Stanley. He'd tried so hard that day to make it nice for everybody, but he always backed down when Gloria turned on him.

Looking downcast, he said quietly, 'I think it's time for bed, boys.'

We didn't have to be told twice. John picked up Davie and the three of us dashed downstairs to the privy and hung about down there for a bit. It was peaceful there because Mrs Stone was away for the day with her family.

We knew it wouldn't take long for Gloria to be dozy enough to ignore us when we returned. As soon as we got back upstairs I dragged my easel into our bedroom and closed the door.

Gloria's turn of mood failed to spoil that Christmas for me. I climbed into bed and pulled the covers up over my ears, leaving my easel on the floor right next to me. I stuck out my hand and touched it. It made me feel as if I was special. I thought of all the pictures I would draw for Stanley. I wanted so much to make him proud of me. I knew he'd got me the best present of all of us and was very happy that he was my Dad.

Chapter Eight

Church bells heralded in the new year. A new school term started; snowdrops finally pushed their heads through the soil, green shoots appeared on trees, the sun chased away grey clouds, spring arrived and my childhood ended.

Rays of early-morning sun fell across my pillow, their warmth touching my face. Still half-asleep I stretched contentedly until the realisation of what had woken me penetrated my brain: Gloria's high-pitched drunken shouting. Nothing unusual in that, but this time I heard something different in her shrill tones: a note of hysteria, of fear and maybe even the dawning awareness that something was about to happen, something she couldn't control. Whatever it was, it frightened me.

A male voice bellowed out, shocking me by its loudness. The words were garbled and indistinguishable. Stanley never raised his voice and the unaccustomed volume made me wonder momentarily if a new uncle had appeared.

The male voice rose and rose until it almost matched the shrill pitch of Gloria's. Then came another sound –

harsh sobs – and with a shock I realised what I didn't want to: they were coming from Stanley.

I turned my head to see John propped on his elbow, just listening. I wanted his wide grin to break out, wanted to be reassured that our world was still all right. But for once there was no smile on his face. He looked almost frightened and the thought of John being frightened made my whole world tilt and my body shake.

Something very bad must be happening.

I looked over to the other side of the room where Davie lay on his put-u-up. He stared back at me with eyes made glassy with the onset of panic.

I knew he wanted to run over and get into bed with us. He was just waiting for me to give him a sign. But I was frozen, unable to move a fraction, even to raise my hand to beckon him.

I heard a noise I recognised from when the uncles called: the scrape of furniture being moved. But this time I sensed that it was not going to be followed by music.

The noise grew fainter and I guessed something was being dragged out to the landing.

And then there was silence; a thick terrifying silence. I reached for John.

I wanted that silence to end, but when it did it was with a scream that was unbearable in its intensity. It was followed by another and another. They bounced against our walls, vibrated in my ears and filled my mind with their horror. I put my hands over my ears to block them out but they forced their way through my fingers. Those screams belonged to Gloria.

John suddenly moved. He flew to the door and opened it. I crawled out of bed and staggered to his side. I wanted to tell him to close the door because I didn't want to see – but then I did.

Stanley was balanced on the wooden banister at the top of the stairs. His body was swaying. In front of him there was a clear drop down to the tiled hallway three floors below. One end of a rope was round his neck and the other end was tied to a ceiling beam.

I saw Stanley's legs shake, his body quiver. I wanted to call out to him and tell him to stay with us but the words remained in my throat. Instead we were quiet; so quiet.

Gloria moved forward. 'Stanley,' she said. 'Don't.'

He jumped.

The thunder of footsteps on the stairs, booming voices and Gloria's screams mingled together and hurt my head. I put my hands over my ears. I wanted the noises to go away.

John shut our door. We sat on the edge of the bed, numb with shock. Davie's tears were welling up but none of us said anything. My mind was a white blank without any thoughts in it.

I've got no idea how long it was before the door of our room opened. Some neighbours were standing there, with Mrs Stone, who was holding Denise.

'He's alive,' someone said. 'They cut him down. They reached him just in time.' Seemingly the clumsily tied knot had failed to break his neck. My panic momentarily receded, but still there was a nagging anxiety. What would happen now? Could things just go back to normal? I had a horrible feeling they couldn't.

Mrs Stone smirked at John. 'Seems Stanley found out about your Ma's gentlemen,' she laughed. 'Silly, pathetic man! He knew what she had been up to in the war. The whole town did. You'll know all about that too, don't you, John?'

'Where is she?' I asked, but no one seemed to know. It seemed that Gloria had disappeared; fled.

No, they didn't know where she had gone; nor were they interested.

'Where's Stanley?' I asked, not daring to look towards the landing where I had last seen him balanced on the banister.

Stanley had gone, they told us, taken away to a hospital by ambulance. Men in white coats had taken him. No, he wasn't coming back either.

Still I felt nothing but blankness; it was as if I was paralysed, beyond feeling.

'You can't stay here,' Mrs Stone told us with barely disguised glee.

One of the neighbours told us to get dressed and said someone was coming to fetch us. We were to stay in our room until they did.

We knew it was useless to argue. Without the freedom that Gloria's indifference had given us, we were children who had to do what adults told us. Children did not have rights.

The voices moved from the landing to the sitting room; there was lots of talking. Straining to hear, we recognised the voices of Mrs Stone and some of the other neighbours but the wails of the baby were so loud that we couldn't make out what the voices were saying. We got dressed in silence, as they had instructed us to do, then we all sat very quietly on our bed, our trembling thighs pressed against each other's. We waited to see what was going to happen. I don't know how long we waited, but it seemed a very long time.

We were brought food: cheese sandwiches and glasses of milk and later some orange squash. They allowed us to go downstairs to the lavatory, but all the time we knew we were being watched. Mrs Stone did not want us disappearing that day.

We heard more noise on the stairs: heavy footfalls and male voices we did not recognise.

'They're in there,' we heard Mrs Stone say as she opened our bedroom door.

Two policemen stepped into the room. They looked stern. One was tall with a black moustache and wisps of dark hair sticking out from under his helmet. The other, who clutched his helmet in his hand, was fat, with carrot-coloured hair and a bad-tempered, flushed face. He wiped the sweat from his eyes as he came into the bedroom. 'Why do they always have to be on the top floor?' he asked no one in particular.

'Get up, boys. You're all going for a little ride. Leave everything behind,' he said when my hand reached to pick up one of my beloved Dinky cars. I looked imploringly at my easel.

'Everything will be sent to you later,' Mrs Stone said, looking down at John with an expression that was almost gleeful. She certainly had no compassion for us; she never had.

We stood up with difficulty. Our knees felt shaky, like jelly. She roughed John's hair with her outstretched, gnarled hand then harshly pushed him in the direction of the policemen.

'Oh John, one more thing …' He looked at her with just a tiny touch of hope in his eyes. 'Whatever story your Ma told you, she lied. There were no American soldiers here during the War. There was only one type – the type your mother liked.' She cackled with delight when she saw his expression change as he took in the meaning of her vicious words. Words I didn't understand then, but they stuck in my head.

The tall, dark officer took John's arm just above the elbow, while the carrot-haired one grabbed me with large fleshy fingers that easily met around my bony wrist. Davie, completely bewildered by the events of the morning, took my other hand and held onto it so tightly that it felt as if he would never let go.

They had sent a black police van for us; it was parked right outside the front door. Other residents of Devonshire Place were gathered round the entrance; the commotion had woken many households that morning. Something had happened and everyone was curious to see

what was going on in their street. I bet they had been speculating and whispering and buzzing with excitement
every time the front door opened.

We were pushed roughly into the back of the van and
the door was slammed shut. The two policemen got in the
front and Mrs Stone passed the squalling baby Denise to
the red-haired one, who wasn't driving. I remember that
her tiny face was almost as red as his big one. There were
no seats in the back for us to sit on; just a wooden bench
that had been designed for grown men, not three small,
frightened children whose feet couldn't reach the floor.
John and I climbed onto it, our legs dangling, then pulled
Davie up and wedged him between us.

That was when he started sobbing. Not for his mother,
certainly not for Stanley, but simply because he was still
only three and three-quarters years old and frightened
almost out of his wits. His mouth opened wide and cries
of terror and bewilderment filled the air. Tears spurted
from his eyes, streamed down his cheeks and blended
with the snot that was trickling from his nose, running
down the sides of his mouth and dripping from his chin.
He gasped for breath between the sobs, choking on occasion so that his face turned scarlet. He looked at me
beseechingly and I, feeling almost as terrified, looked
across at John. I wanted him to say something, anything,
as long as it made it all right. John was my big brother, my
hero. I wanted him to give me that special smile; the one
that told me it was him and me against the world of
grown-ups.

But when I saw the John he had become, in just the few hours between the closing of the door on the familiar world of our childhood and being locked in the van, my fear intensified. My shoulders shook, my legs trembled, my stomach churned. I wanted to pee. I wanted to go home. I wanted to get out of the black van. The boy I knew and looked up to seemed to be disappearing before my eyes, eaten up with a nameless fear that as yet I didn't understand. My brother, my big brother, was sitting on the bench, his head clutched in his hands and his body as slack and defeated as a little old man's.

'John!' I said despairingly. He turned to look at me with eyes that were wide and unfocused. Suddenly they seemed to redden and well up and a tear trickled down his left cheek; just one.

And when I saw his fear, my mouth opened and I sobbed and sobbed.

Our pitiful cries mingled with the wails from the front of the van. Our baby sister, hearing our distress, had pushed her infant's vocal cords to the very limit.

'Shut up, shut your grizzling, the lot of you!' yelled the fat policeman, shaking Denise slightly.

We didn't, we couldn't; only John, John who always had something clever or brave to say, was quiet.

'Shut up, you bloody little bastards,' shouted the other policeman. He turned in the driver's seat to look round and glare at us.

After what seemed like a long journey the van turned sharply, braked and came to a sudden halt. My bottom slid off the wooden bench, then we heard the front doors slam and heavy footsteps approaching the back of the van. The door was wrenched open abruptly, revealing the two policemen. The fat one was clutching our sister roughly as if she was a muddy rugby ball, holding her firmly against his bulky body. The other one reached in at great speed, grabbed John by the neck of his jumper and pulled him out; it was as if he was reaching for an unwanted puppy that had been thrown into the pound rather than a boy.

'John!' I screamed.

'You stay there, you little bastard,' the carrot-haired one shouted at me. But with one man holding a screaming baby and the other a wriggling boy, for just a few seconds they had no free hands between them – a situation I quickly took advantage of. I was already on my feet after the abrupt stop and my legs suddenly gained strength as I flung myself out of that open van door. I was going to get John, to help him, to make him strong again.

I started kicking the policeman who was holding John but he took no notice of me.

A third policeman came running up and laughed at his colleagues when he saw what was happening. 'For God's sake!' he exclaimed. 'Can you boys not control three kids? Here, I'll deal with this one.' He grabbed hold of John's arm. 'He's going straight to Haut de la Garenne, right?'

'Right,' was the answer.

Hearing it confirmed, the third policeman twisted John's arm until it was behind his back. I heard him say,

'No nonsense now, you little bugger. You struggle any more and your arm will break.' Holding him firmly in that grip, he propelled him forward, away from us.

I tried to run after them but my arms were being pulled tightly back until I was bent almost double. I yelled, I struggled and I dug my heels into the ground, but all to no avail. I was picked up, swung into the air and thrown back into the van. My bottom landed on the wooden bench with such a forceful thump that it nearly made me bounce right back out again.

Past the bulky shapes of the policemen I watched in horror as John was hurled forcefully into another black van, like a sack of Jersey Royal potatoes being loaded at the docks. The door was slammed shut and I couldn't see him any more. I knew they had taken him away from us and in despair I banged my head against the side of the van and yelled out in anguish and frustration.

Davie's whole body shook as he clung to my leg. The last few minutes had shocked him into silence and temporarily stifled his sobs but they didn't stop mine. The tears spurted from my eyes and I thought about the times when John had seen my eyes well up, usually after I had tripped and fallen hard. On those occasions he had sternly told me, 'Big boys don't cry.' But that day I knew I wasn't a big boy and neither was John. I was five and a half and terrified.

'Where's my brother? Where are you taking him?' I screamed at the policemen. They ignored me and got back into the van. I sobbed louder until the whole vehicle vibrated with my misery. Baby Denise picked up on my anguish and with one extra-loud wail she added her little voice to the lament.

'Shut up!' the driver shouted, banging the wire mesh that separated us boys from them. 'Just shut up, you little buggers.' And more from a sudden overwhelming lack of energy than obedience, my sobs faded.

'Look, son,' he said then. 'We're taking you somewhere you'll be looked after. For your own sake, just be good and calm down. There's a nice evening meal waiting for you where you're going.'

I repeated that I just wanted my older brother.

'You'll all meet up later, so stop your nonsense now,' he said, and promise after promise rolled off his tongue. Those policemen would have promised us anything if it meant they could keep us from crying.

But through the grille I spotted the telltale winks when they made those promises and saw the merriment on their faces; I heard their barely suppressed chuckles and knew that they were lying to us.

Davie and I were too drained to offer any more resistance and for the rest of that journey we huddled up to each other and sat in miserable silence. Even Denise seemed to have run out of energy and she just snuffled softly in the policeman's arms.

The van slowed down and gradually came to a halt. A few seconds later the back doors were swung open. 'Out you get, boys,' said the tall, dark policeman.

It was mid-afternoon and the strong Jersey sunlight flooded in, momentarily blinding me. I put my hand up to shield my eyes from the sun's glare. With a derisive snort the policeman caught hold of my wrist, jerked it hard and pulled me out.

'I said out, you little moron. Can't you ever do as you're told? Let me tell you, in here you'll have to.' He chuckled as though at a joke, one that judging from his colleague's answering snigger both of them understood the full meaning of. Young as I was, I instantly knew that joke was at our expense.

'Do you know where you are, Robbie?' asked the carrot-haired policeman, this time not too unkindly.

By then speech had deserted me and all I could do was shake my lowered head.

'Sacre Coeur, or Sacred Heart to you, you little heathens.'

The name meant nothing to me. I still had no idea why we had been taken from our home or why we had been brought to this place. I understood that what Stanley had done was bad, but why were we all being punished? And where had Gloria gone? Even more to the point, where had they taken John?

His next words made even less sense. 'This is going to be your new home, and by all accounts a lot better than the one you lot came from.'

I just wanted to be back in Devonshire Place. Back with Gloria and Mrs Stone's familiar shouts, slaps and moans.

The tall, dark policeman lifted Davie down from the van. The moment his feet touched firm ground he started crying again. Tired, hiccuping sounds left his mouth while fat tears slid down his flushed cheeks and his round little-boy body trembled all over.

My eyes widened as I stared around me, trying to take in and make sense of our surroundings.

We were standing in front of the biggest building I had ever seen. Built of stone, it had been painted a dark cream colour. My red-rimmed eyes were drawn upwards, up and up the five storeys of the building until they came to the roof. On top of it was a huge statue. It frightened me. I didn't know that the stone man with his arms outstretched to the sky was the same Jesus that I had been taught about at school. This eight-foot-tall figure was not the gentle man we had been told about in our Bible class. This statue looked macabre and threatening.

Then I noticed that the high walls surrounding the buildings had sharp, dangerous-looking spikes embedded in the top, adding to the intimidating atmosphere. A shiver of apprehension travelled up my spine and I felt the sharp bite of fear.

I was too dazed and far too upset to take in more of what the grounds and the buildings actually looked like. I just got the impression of its vastness, then my arm was grabbed again. We were swiftly marched up to the big double front door and a distant bell could be heard ringing.

The policeman who carried our baby sister was holding her as far away from him as possible. I could smell the ripe stink of her nappy and her wails of outrage, hunger and discomfort rose shrilly into the air. I could sense the policemen's impatience and knew they just wanted to hand us over as quickly as possible. But who, I wondered, were they handing us over to?

Chapter Nine

The door was opened by a woman wearing a thick, black dress that came to just above her ankles. Her head was covered in the same black material and her face was framed in what looked like a huge white collar. Around her waist she wore a thick leather belt with a large bunch of keys and a crucifix hanging from it.

For the first time I looked up into the pale face of Sister Bernadette. I saw thin lips pressed firmly together and small dark eyes, lacking warmth and humour, that were staring back down at us. I felt my own eyes widen. Her white wimple completely hid every strand of hair, removing any sign of femininity, while her long black veil obscured the sides of her cheeks and gave an almost sinister quality to her unsmiling face.

I felt Davie grip my hand tighter and knew he was afraid of her. Neither of us had ever seen a nun before, and I felt a wave of panic at the sight of this strangely dressed woman.

She looked at the policeman. 'These must be the Garner children,' she said in a tone of indifference. 'You had better bring them in.'

She ushered us quickly into a large marble-floored hall. Davie gave a gasp and clutched my arm. My eyes followed his frightened gaze. In front of me was another statue, only this time its chest looked as though it had been ripped open to expose a heart dripping with blood. At the sight of it Davie shook with fresh sobs.

'We don't allow crying here,' the nun said, ignoring our distress. She cast an icy gaze over the weeping Davie. She didn't raise her voice; she didn't need to. The coldness and authority of her words were enough: 'Be quiet immediately.'

I heard Davie gulp. His crying tailed off until all I could hear were shallow little gasping breaths. I looked down at him. I wanted to tell him that everything was going to be all right but I didn't believe that myself. My heart shifted when I saw how great a toll the day had taken on him. His mottled red face was covered with silvery tracks; so many tears had flowed that it looked as if an acid substance had burnt its path down his chubby cheeks. His eyelids were so swollen that they were almost closed shut. His mouth drooped with fright and bewilderment and he leant against me as though he had lost the ability to stand unaided.

The nun in front of us remained completely unmoved at the sight of two small boys who for hours had been traumatised, bewildered and frightened. That eventful spring morning we had woken up to the sounds of our mother's screams and witnessed Stanley's attempted suicide, then we had been removed from our home, seemingly abandoned by the only parents we knew, and finally we had been roughly and harshly separated from our eldest brother John, the boy who did everything for us and who we regarded more as a parent-protector than a brother.

I recognised the nun's antipathy towards us and the recognition of it ignited a tiny spark of defiance in me. 'Where's John?' I asked. Her eyes flicked over me and in their depths I saw a mixture of contempt and enjoyment of the predicament we found ourselves in.

'He's not here,' was her reply.

'Where is he?' I repeated.

She paused and for a moment it seemed that she was not even going to grant me a reply for she just stared unblinkingly back at me. This time I held her gaze for I wanted an answer.

'Somewhere naughty boys like him go,' she said eventually. 'Your landlady told the police what he was like. Trouble, we heard. A criminal in the making. Always stealing off the shopkeepers, wasn't he? We don't want that sort of boy here. So if you know what's good for you, forget him and stop asking questions about him.'

I dropped my gaze then. That tiny spark of defiance that had flickered within me was totally extinguished by her words. I'd always thought the shopkeepers didn't know about John's thieving but I suppose they must have seen him sometimes even if they hadn't caught him. Surely he hadn't been sent somewhere we couldn't see him? Surely that wasn't true? But I knew it was; deep down I had known when I saw him being put into the other police van that I might not see him ever again.

When I raised my eyes and looked at the black-gowned figure, sheer panic froze my vocal cords. A huge lump rose in my throat, threatening to stop me breathing; I gulped and gulped again, trying as hard as I could to draw fresh breath into my lungs. All the time I gasped for air, Sister Bernadette watched me with a look of malevolent pleasure.

Another nun appeared as if from nowhere.

'Ah, Sister Freda,' she said. 'Please relieve the policeman of the baby.' With a look of relief the policeman passed over our sister.

'She needs changing,' Sister Freda said as she took her from him and left with a swish of her black robes.

That was yet another family member I lost that day.

Their duty done, the two policemen left quickly after that, but we still hadn't been told what was going to happen to us. Sister Bernadette watched them go without saying a word, while we stood in front of her wondering what would happen next.

'Follow me,' she said abruptly. She turned and walked briskly towards a door set at the rear of the entrance hall. I pulled Davie along with me as I half-walked and half-ran, trying to keep up with her short, thickset figure moving swiftly in front of us. She never once glanced back to see if we could keep up. As I followed, the fear that I had felt for Mrs Stone seemed infinitesimal compared to the growing terror that this nun induced.

If she scared me, the building, with its long gloomy passages, closed doors, statues standing in corners and morbid pictures of the crucifixion hanging on walls, absolutely terrified me. Smells of floor polish mixed with the odour of stale air for, as I was to find out, Sacre Coeur's rooms very seldom had windows flung open to allow fresh air to enter. This added to its depressing atmosphere, as did the eerie silence.

The sister unlocked a heavy wooden door that led into a courtyard and then led us through to a tarmac yard. 'This is the girls' play area,' she told us. 'The only time you are allowed in it is when you are going to the boys' dining room. The girls have their own refectory.'

I found out later that the girls were always sent in to have their meals before us so that our paths never crossed.

'When you've had your supper you had better learn your way about,' she continued. 'The yard on the other side of the hedge is the boys' play area. There is another door, which is unlocked after supper, that leads into it. You are never to enter the girls' area except at meal times. Do you understand me?'

'What about our sister?' I asked despairingly. 'When do we get to see her?'

She ignored the question. 'Robbie, I asked you if you understood what I've just told you. Have I been wasting my breath?'

I was too intimidated to dare ask about Denise again. Instead I just told her that I understood what she had been saying to me. I could see that the courtyard we were walking through was encircled on all sides by the massive building we had arrived in, and I could also see the hedge crossing the middle of that courtyard.

She opened another wooden door and led us into a long, narrow room where about sixty boys were sitting on benches at long tables. I was relieved to see some other children and to realise that this must be a dining room, so chances were we would get fed soon. The walls were painted the dreary green of bruised apples and the floor was covered with dark brown lino. There had been a low murmur of talking as we walked in but the boys fell completely silent when they saw Sister Bernadette.

'What have I told you?' she said sharply to the room at large. 'There is to be no talking until after the meal.'

She pointed to two empty places. 'That is where you are to sit, but first stand behind the bench and say your grace.'

Davie and I looked at each other, puzzled. I had to tell her we didn't know the words of any grace. She gave an exasperated sigh and glanced along the table as though looking for inspiration. Her chilly gaze landed on a thin, wiry boy with curly, light-brown hair and a snub-nosed face liberally dotted with freckles, who was sitting next to the place I had been told was mine.

'Ah, Nicolas,' she ordered. 'Say your grace again and they can repeat the words after you.'

'Yes, sister,' the boy replied without looking at us.

'And after supper you can show them around, then bring them to mass.'

He looked up at us then. 'Yes, sister,' he replied obediently and gave me a slight smile.

'Good. I'll leave them in your charge for the rest of today. You're responsible for them.'

Her gown brushed the floor as she turned and walked briskly out of the room, taking with her some of the tension that her presence had caused.

Nicolas climbed off the bench, stood behind it and hurriedly said grace. I repeated the words after him.

'Better try and remember them,' he told me with a quick grin.

I reckoned he was roughly three years older than me. There was something about him that reminded me of some of John's friends. He had the air of a boy who'd had to live on his wits and I also knew, before he said anything, that he sympathised with our misery. His presence gave me some comfort that first bewildering evening. I sat down with him on one side of me and Davie on the other.

There was a clatter of metal plates at a nearby counter and another nun, much older and thinner than Sister Bernadette, started ladling food onto them from a large pot. As soon as we were seated she pushed two tin plates in front of Davie and me. They held a thin stew that consisted of gristly grey meat, cabbage and potatoes; its surface was spotted with white flecks of congealing fat. The smell of overcooked cabbage seemed to seep out of the walls, as well as from our plates. It mingled with the sour smell of the room as though the air was filled with the lingering stench of the thousands of miserable meals that had been consumed there.

'Eat!' snapped the old nun. I looked down at the unappetising mess on my plate and shook my head as I pushed the plate to one side. Watching me, Davie did the same. I didn't want to be at that place or at that table. I didn't want that food that looked and smelled so horrible. I knew if I put anything in my mouth it wouldn't get past the lump that was still so firmly wedged in my throat.

'This once,' said the nun, perhaps noting our despondency, 'I'll overlook your behaviour, but don't expect me to do so again. You must eat the food God blesses you with.'

As she moved away, Nicolas whispered that I'd had a lucky escape. 'See that ladle she carries? She hits you with it. Bloody old witch, that one. It's only because it's your first day she didn't lam into you. Just be careful of her, she's going a bit dilly. She's deaf as a doorpost too. But the one you really have to watch out for is Sister Bernadette. You never want her to notice you doing wrong.' He must have noticed my fearful expression and hastened to add some reassurance. 'But don't worry, I'll show you the ropes. You'll be OK with me.'

Davie had heard the whispered words and the build-up of terror he had felt all day suddenly became too much for him to cope with. He put his hands on the table for leverage, started rocking himself backwards and forwards and howled loudly. The old nun turned round, glared at our table and scurried towards us.

'Try and stop him,' Nicolas hissed, a note of panic in his voice.

But it was too late to silence him before the old nun reached us. Quivering with outrage at our effrontery, she screamed that we had committed a cardinal sin. Firstly, for not eating what had been put in front of us. 'Food,' she shrieked, 'that starving children in Africa would have been grateful of.' Her rage increased with every screech and howl that left Davie's throat. Secondly, she told us that nobody made a noise like that in her domain. Thirdly, Davie had placed not just his hands on the table but his elbows as well; both these actions were firmly against Sacre Coeur's rules of behaviour. 'Don't think these sinful acts will go unpunished,' she said, her rage bubbling over.

She swung the large metal ladle above her head to gain maximum force behind the forthcoming blow. I was scared that the weight of that ladle would crush or break Davie's arm and in an attempt to protect him I started to get up from the bench.

Well aware of the damage that could be inflicted on my little brother, Nicolas reacted without thinking of the consequences. He placed his hand on the table, leaned across me and knocked Davie's arms down to his sides. The ladle changed direction in mid-air and with a sudden crack it connected with Nicolas's outstretched hand. He screamed in agony. The nun lifted her other arm and swiped him so hard across the side of his head that he fell with a deafening crash to the floor.

Davie stopped howling, his eyes wide with shock, and his face turned from red to white in seconds. Surreptitiously he slipped his thumb into his mouth.

'That will teach you to interfere,' the nun said with smug satisfaction when she saw the pain Nicolas was in. She turned her watery blue eyes onto us. I saw no spark of intelligence in that gaze; she looked old and senile, and utterly without any sympathy for the helpless children in her care.

'And not another peep out of you or your brother, do you hear? If you can't behave around others I'll have to talk to Sister Bernadette about putting you on your own for a while.'

Having delivered her threat, she walked off in search of other victims. Nicolas clambered back onto to the bench cradling his bruised hand. He didn't utter a word until she was out of earshot, then he muttered, 'You'd better be careful. She means it. They put you in a dark cupboard. Leave you there. Just give you bread and water. I've been in it.'

I hoped Davie couldn't hear him. The last thing I wanted was for him to start crying again. I knew if he did I would get blamed as much as him. But this time he kept quiet, just sucking his thumb for comfort.

Chapter Ten

When the bell rang the boys rose up almost as one body. Once again they stood behind the benches, bent their heads, closed their eyes and chanted their prayers thanking the Holy Mother for their supper. Nicolas nudged me, indicating we should do the same. I moved my lips hoping that the old nun would think I was saying the right words. When they had done they stacked their plates, folded their napkins and then, row by row, turned on their heels and filed out in total silence.

Once outside in the early evening sunshine, Nicolas started firing questions at me. 'So why are you here? Haven't you got a dad? Is he dead or something? What about your mother?' He didn't pause for breath or wait for answers between each question.

'I dunno. I dunno why they put us here.' I felt the tears welling up again. 'My mum and dad aren't dead. My dad's sick, though.'

I knew Stanley must be ill because I'd heard a policeman say he was sick in the head.

'If they're not dead they'll come for you, won't they?'

Why hadn't I thought of that? Gloria wouldn't just leave us here, would she? Wasn't Stanley always good to me? So as soon as he was well they would come. Wouldn't they?

My new friend paraphrased my thoughts as though he had read my mind. 'Well then, when he's better they'll come for you. You're lucky; mine are both dead. Maybe I'll get adopted, though.'

'What do you mean?' I asked. Adopt wasn't a word I'd heard before.

'It's when grown-ups want to get a child. They come and look at us and decide which one of us they like best. Then we go and live in their house. We have our own bedroom and a bicycle and a puppy. But they only want to take children who look happy, so I always smile at them.'

I looked at the hope in my new friend's face, but instead of feeling the same emotion I felt a sinking feeling in the pit of my stomach.

What would happen if Gloria and Stanley didn't come for us? What if Davie and I got taken away by one of these couples who wanted someone else's children? How would John find us if we were taken away? I didn't like the idea that we could be adopted.

Then another worrying thought came into my mind. 'What happens if they only want to adopt one little boy?'

Nicolas immediately understood the meaning behind my question and said, 'You'd tell them you were two boys, a pair, not just the one. They only want to take boys who are happy, so when they come, make sure you are together and smiling. Tell them you are brothers and you must look after Davie. Maybe they'd like two boys.'

Seeing that I still looked unconvinced, Nicolas quickly added, 'Still, if your mum and dad are coming to get you when your dad's better, you can't just go off with them.' Seeing that both Davie and I looked as if we were on the verge of tears, he gave up talking about adoption and asking searching questions.

'Come on,' he urged, pointing to an outbuilding that was joined to the main building by a covered walkway. 'That's where the lavatories and the washrooms are. Let's get down to them quickly. We want to get there before everyone else.'

As he hurried towards the brick outbuilding in that uncoordinated lope peculiar to young boys, especially those wearing badly fitting shoes, I wondered why he was in such a hurry. He hadn't said anything earlier about being desperate for a pee. But when I got there, I realised that you wouldn't want to be the last one in the queue and have to wait for a space at a urinal or for a cubicle to become empty.

The moment we walked in, the stench of piss and shit attacked my nostrils, making my stomach heave and my eyes water. The uproar of boys jeering and clamouring as they fought their way to the urinals and cubicles filled my ears. Big boys shoved the smaller ones out of the way as they pushed forward. Cubicle doors were pounded the moment someone got inside, whilst shouts of 'Hurry up, I want to go!' bounced off the walls. Small boys clutched themselves through the front of their short trousers as, with crossed legs and bent bodies, they jigged desperately from side to side trying not to pee in their pants.

To the right there was a row of urinals too high for Davie or me to use. Wash-hand basins lined the left wall while the cubicles were facing us as we entered – just five cubicles for sixty boys.

We stood in the pushing, wriggling scrum of what passed for a queue and were jostled every few seconds by some larger boy whose need was clearly desperate.

'Want to go now, Robbie,' Davie said, uttering the first words he had spoken for most of that long day.

'Don't wet yourself,' I begged, for Davie was not used to having to wait when he wanted to go. Something told me that in this place peeing yourself would be a punishable offence.

Nicolas saw our plight and pushed us quickly forward at the precise moment a boy came out of a cubicle.

'Go on in. You both go, I'm all right. I'll use those,' he said, jerking his hand in the direction of the urinals, which were nearly hidden by the mass of small boys using them, often three at a time using the same urinal.

Almost limp with gratitude, I closed the door, then bile rose in my throat when I saw the inside of the cubicle. Fat bluebottles buzzed above my head, and if the smell outside had been bad, the stench inside was indescribable. Lumps of faeces and clumps of soiled toilet paper clung to the sides of the lavatory, turds floated on the surface of it and yards of that hard transparent toilet paper, so popular in institutions, trailed in the puddles of urine that splattered the floor.

Davie pulled his pants down and tried to hold them up with his knees. He placed both his hands on the broken wooden seat and gingerly sat on them, trying to stop his legs coming into contact with the filthy wet seat. He finished and climbed down, his shorts bottoms wet from the mess on the floor.

There was loud banging on the door. 'Get a move on in there!' shouted a voice, and another one joined in. 'Come on or we'll break the bleeding door down.' My fear at that loud angry voice almost stopped me being able to finish peeing.

The area where we washed our hands was hardly any better. The stained basins were beyond grimy and the floor, trampled by sixty pairs of feet several times a day, was smeared with filth. The smell from the nearby urinals was sour and pungent. All of a sudden that outside privy in Devonshire Place, with its neatly cut-up squares of newspaper and its neatly tiled floor, seemed luxurious by comparison.

I washed my hands, then found there was no soap and the soiled roller towel was broken. I just shook them dry, ran them through my hair and went outside to wait for Nicolas.

Davie's head drooped sleepily. He wanted to sit down. 'I'm tired, Robbie,' he said plaintively. 'Want to go to bed.'

'He can't,' Nicolas told me when he appeared. 'We have to go to chapel now. If we're late we get into big trouble with the nuns.'

'What sort of trouble?' I asked.

'Whopped with that leather strap they carry – or even worse, that belt they always wear. Seen the buckle on it? You don't want to feel that, I can tell you. Sister Bernadette, she's the worst. She likes hitting us.' Grabbing Davie's hand, he helped me to pull him along.

Without his help that day, what would we have done? We were so grateful that he even managed to earn a trusting, watery smile from Davie.

I had never been inside a church before, although this was something I thought it best not to admit. I did know that we weren't Catholics or 'Left-footers', as Gloria had always called them disparagingly.

I told Nicolas that and he looked at me with astonishment. 'Don't be stupid, Robbie. Everyone in here is or becomes Catholic. Sister Bernadette makes sure of that.'

'How?' I asked.

'She'll turn you into one, make you read stuff, say all them prayers and things. Now stop asking questions,' he said good-naturedly, before I could tell him I wasn't very good at reading yet and had never been taught to say my prayers.

It was only when we reached the doors of the chapel that I saw the girls who lived in the orphanage for the first time. Wearing long grey skirts with matching baggy jumpers and thick stockings, their eyes were cast demurely downwards, avoiding contact with ours. They walked in a straggly crocodile with a nun bringing up the rear.

'Shush,' whispered Nicolas when I pointed them out. 'We're not allowed to speak to them. Not ever.'

'But my sister is in here. She's a baby.'

He gave me a pitying look. 'If she's a baby, she won't be here long.'

I asked him what he meant but all he would say was that I would find out for myself. I wondered if there was another place where they took babies, just until they grew up a bit more.

Then we were inside. The girls sat on the left facing the altar, the boys on the right. And all the time we were in there, I was conscious of the nuns, two for us and two for the girls, scanning our faces and looking for any sign of disrespect, any sign of a small child falling asleep, or any giggling, talking or smiling – in fact any sins that would give them an excuse to punish us later.

Nicolas and I propped Davie between us. I felt my eyes begin to close as the sounds of the priest's monotonous voice droned hypnotically on. The words were in Latin and had no meaning to me and my body sagged with tiredness. Dimly I listened to the sermon that at least was in English. I felt my body roll sideways and my eyelids grow heavy. Seeing my eyes flicker shut Nicolas nudged me hard in the ribs and mouthed a warning: 'Stay awake.' I dug my nails into my hands trying to stop my eyes closing again and concentrated on prodding Davie, who was dangerously close to sleep.

I saw one little boy about Davie's age, his thin face white with concentration and his huge unblinking eyes stretched wide as if matchsticks had been inserted to keep them open. He stared straight in front of him but gradually tiredness overcame him, his head drooped, his eyes fluttered shut and his small body swayed forward in the pew. From just behind him a pair of hands shot out and pushed hard in between his shoulder blades. There was a loud thump as he fell forwards, hitting his head on the pew in front. It was as if no one heard the noise; it was completely ignored.

The boy looked dazed as he picked himself up but instead of crying, which I expected him to, he just wrapped his arms around his body protectively, fixed his enormous eyes on the priest and sat silently for the rest of the service.

At last the priest gave what I learnt was the benediction. In his hand he held a golden cross, and he moved it across his body and raised it in the air as he gave his blessing.

I watched the choir follow the priest towards the doors, then the nuns and finally the altar boys who, like the nuns, were dressed in black and white. Still that little boy sat frozen, without a scrap of emotion on his face. I found that my eyes were constantly drawn to him.

When it was time to go outside, Nicolas said we had an hour free before getting ready for bed. The little boy just stood in a corner of the yard, still with his arms hugging his body, staring at something only he could see. He was a skinny scrap of a thing with dark hair and bright blue eyes.

'His name's Jimmy,' Nicolas told me. His mother had died a few months earlier giving birth. The baby was born dead. His father had gone to England to work. There were no other relatives to care for him so he had been put in the orphanage. When visitors came he stared at them, then looked away once he realised that his dad was not among them. This disappointment was to be repeated many, many times for Jimmy's father never came.

I was dropping with tiredness but we had to sit through half an hour's religious studies before we were allowed to have a wash and go to bed. By this time Davie was only semi-conscious and I had to half-drag him up the stairs. We followed the crowd to a dormitory, somehow pulled on the sets of pyjamas that were handed to us, and crawled into the beds we were shown to. Exhaustion wiped out the events of the day and I fell mercifully asleep.

Chapter Eleven

On my first morning at Sacre Coeur the unmistakable wails of a baby woke me even before the sun had risen. For a few seconds I thought it was Denise and, believing I was at home in Devonshire Place, I stretched and reached my arm over to shake John awake – but my hand touched only air.

I sat up in the bed and realised that I was in the middle of a row of beds and on the opposite side of the room was a matching row. Between us were babies' cots arranged in a circle and it was from one of them that the cries were coming.

The sound rose, the cries turning into howls of outrage at being ignored. Then I saw a boy of around ten crawling from his bed and going over to the cot. He lifted the baby out, carried him over to his bed and laid him down. I wondered if Denise might be there, so I ran over to have a look but there were only two other cots there and neither of the sleeping babies was her. 'I'm looking for my baby sister. We arrived yesterday,' I said to the boy who had picked up the baby. 'She'll be in the girls' section,' he whispered.

I learnt later that the very young babies, some virtually newborns, were looked after in a nursery that was located in the girls' section, but once they slept straight through the night the baby boys were brought into our dormitory. At night, before lights out, a large metal pot was boiled in the sick bay, glass bottles were sterilised and the last feed was prepared. They were given to the babies by one of the nuns, assisted by several of the boys who were aged ten or over. The same routine was followed in the morning. They were given their first feed of the day shortly after five-thirty, which was the time the orphanage sprang into life.

That first morning as I watched the boy with his small charge, the events of the previous day came rushing back. I wanted to cry as loudly as that baby but I already knew that if I did no one would come to comfort me.

A bell rang. Boys threw back the bedclothes and jumped out onto the cold floor. Davie remained curled in the foetal position under his covers. I went over to him.

'Come on, wake up!' I tried to pull him up but he just lay there, refusing to open his scrunched-up eyes and look at me.

His thumb was in his mouth and tears ran down his cheeks, which already seemed to have lost their plumpness. When I put my hand out to touch him he felt feverishly hot and clammy.

I was too intent on trying to persuade Davie to get up to hear the footsteps approaching our beds and I jumped with fright when I heard a woman's voice, sharp with anger, addressing my little brother. She spoke so close to my ear that I could feel her breath on the back of my neck.

'Get out of bed now.'

Davie's body twitched but he made no sound and didn't attempt to sit up. Fear slithered up and down my spine and I looked round to see Sister's Bernadette's second-in-command, Sister Freda, glaring down at us.

'Either he gets out on his own or I'll pull him out and, believe me, he won't like me doing that,' she told me angrily.

'Davie, please,' I pleaded frantically. 'Please get up.' Somehow the fear in my voice penetrated his pitiful lethargy. Without speaking, he slid out of bed and leant sleepily against me, his fingers seeking out my own.

'First of all,' she said, 'you have to learn how to make your own beds.' She showed us how to make sure the sheets were pulled tight, that not a crease showed and that the corners were tucked neatly in. 'You will do this every morning. Now come with me,' she said.

Davie and I were still wearing the faded pyjamas we had been issued with the night before. Did she want us to get dressed or come as we were? She hadn't said and I looked up at her, worried and confused. She sighed with impatience at what she obviously saw as my stupidity.

'You've both got to get your uniforms, so you can come as you are. Hurry up now. I've not got all day.' With an irritated sniff she turned and walked briskly away. Clutching my pyjamas for fear they might drop down in our haste, we followed her down the passageway into the washroom.

'These are yours,' she told us as we entered the cold, high-ceilinged room, handing us each a small pile consisting of a red facecloth, a bar of strong-smelling carbolic soap, a toothbrush and a tin of Gibbs pink tooth powder which, when mixed with water, turned into a paste. Finally there was a washbag to keep everything in. She indicated a numbered hook on the wall where we could hang our things. Davie's number was 18 and mine, close by, was 20.

She pointed to large buckets of water placed alongside a smaller bucket and some tin bowls. She told us to use the small bucket to scoop water from the larger one, then we could pour it into the tin bowls and wash our faces, necks and hands.

I looked at the brownish cold water which had, unbeknown to me, been brought up from the well earlier that morning by the senior boys, and I recoiled from it. I didn't want to dip my toothbrush in that muddy liquid, but then I thought of the grim expression on Sister Freda's face and reluctantly started to wet my facecloth.

Once we had washed to her satisfaction, she sat first me then Davie on a straight-backed chair. She produced a large pair of rusting scissors and swiftly cut our hair so short that our scalps showed through it.

Next we were kitted out in the Sacre Coeur uniform – a uniform so distinctively ugly that no matter where we went there could be no mistaking where we had come from. First we were given our underpants and vests and pairs of long, thick woollen socks with hardened darn

marks on the heel. I pulled these on and helped Davie
with his and waited until the Sister passed us a pair of
coarsely woven, grey woollen short trousers. They were so
absurdly baggy that perhaps in different circumstances we
might have collapsed in giggles. The woollen jumpers
were in almost as bad a condition as those cast-offs of
John's that Gloria had given me when I started school
about six months earlier. Lastly, she handed us our boots.
Made of thick, scuffed black leather, they came halfway
up our calves and laced down the front, and neither pair
fitted us very well.

'Those you will polish every day before morning mass,'
she told us, as she led Davie and me back into the main
marble-tiled entrance hall and showed us a large
cupboard tucked under the stairs, where polish and old
pairs of boots were kept. She unlocked it and passed us a
tin of black boot polish and a dirty rag. I remembered
Nicolas saying that the nuns sometimes locked you in a
dark cupboard and I shuddered, wondering if this might
be the one.

Next we went to morning mass, which we were told
took place at seven-thirty every morning in the chapel that
took over the ground floor on one side of the massive
building. As we walked across the courtyard the sun
hadn't fully risen. Nuns appeared through various doors,
their black veils flapping like the wings of giant birds and
the keys that hung from their belts clinking at every step
they took. To my child's eyes they appeared as dark spirits, moving down gloomy corridors.

At eight-fifteen we all queued outside the mess room until the door was unlocked, showed the sister in charge the cleanliness of our hands, entered silently, said grace and gulped down our breakfast, a bowl of revolting watery porridge. We then stacked our dirty plates and carried them into the kitchen.

Next we were told we would be given chores each day. We should change our boots for thick outside ones if we were working in the acres of vegetable gardens that stretched out in front of the buildings, or in the green-houses or the dark litter barns where hundreds of chick-ens were bred behind the orphanage. If we were working inside, in the kitchens or the laundry that were on the opposite side of the courtyard from the chapel, we were to wear knitted slippers.

I don't remember what jobs Davie and I did that first day. We tried to keep our heads down and obey orders, petrified as we saw children all around us being punished harshly for minor misdemeanours. I listened hard to what the nuns said, hoping to avoid punishment myself, but I soon realised they believed that all the chil-dren at the orphanage, even newborn babies, had been conceived in sin and were contaminated. They further believed that these children should be punished for the sins of their mothers and fathers. In fact it was the holy duty of the nuns to punish by rod, strap or birch any child who had an impure thought or had committed an act of disrespect to man, woman or, most importantly, God.

'Your father tried to kill himself,' one nun told me, 'and that's a mortal sin.' I worried that I was going to be punished because of Stanley's actions. How could I know if I was committing an act of disrespect when I didn't know anything about their religion? It was all very confusing.

That evening followed the same routine as the previous one. At five-thirty we had our supper, then we had an hour to queue up for the lavatories, breathe in fresh air and get to mass. After mass we had half an hour of religious study, then at quarter to nine there was a rush to the washrooms, and nine o'clock was bedtime.

That first day was the beginning of a routine that seldom varied. And as the months passed in Sacre Coeur, I didn't want it changed; change, as I quickly learnt, was seldom safe.

Chapter Twelve

On our second day at Sacre Coeur, Sister Freda approached me at breakfast. I was trying to choke down my porridge when she said: 'Robbie, we all know that the Devil finds work for idle hands.' I looked at her uncomprehendingly. 'So we have arranged some work for you, and you can bring your little brother as well.' Still I stared blankly at her, unsure what she meant. Her voice grew shrill with the beginnings of anger. 'There's no place here for lazy little boys,' she snapped, and I wondered why she was getting cross when we hadn't done anything wrong.

Davie sat silently at my side. His hand clutched my arm and his chubby little body, which seemed to have shrunk over the last forty-eight hours, pressed against mine. I felt his utter, bewildered misery and my eyes began to water but a sense of self-preservation stopped me from crying. Instead I swallowed hard.

Obediently we climbed off our bench and followed Sister Freda along dark corridors and through a door we hadn't seen before that opened onto the boys' playground. We crossed over the tarmac square and took a path that led to an outhouse.

Sister Freda knocked on the door. As it swung open, I came face to face with a grossly fat man who terrified me at first sight. He had a bulbous nose, thick rubbery lips and pale small eyes framed by sparse fair eyelashes.

'Good morning, Neville,' she said.

He answered her politely while regarding me appraisingly. His eyes darted over my body before looking into my face and as my eyes met his I recognised something in their depths: a gloating lewdness, an anticipation of something I had no name for, both mixed together in an expression that somehow repulsed me.

'Here are two new boys, Robbie and Davie,' she said. 'Get them both to help you. Davie's not so young that he can't do anything.' She cast her frosty gaze down onto us. 'I don't want to hear any complaints about you two. You are to do what Neville tells you. You heard what I said – that little brother of yours is to pull his weight here too.'

'But Sister, he's not four yet!' I exclaimed.

As the words left my mouth I wanted to swallow them back for I knew they were a mistake.

Sister Freda, who was jealously aware of her position as second in command, had no tolerance for any word or action that appeared to question her authority. Her face darkened with rage, and she raised her arm and swished the leather strap she was holding across the backs of my legs.

'Don't you answer me back, you child of the Devil!' she screeched.

I gasped with pain and shock, my legs stinging from the blow. Her arm rose again and I lifted one of mine to protect my head. She caught hold of it, held me tightly and brought that thick strap down across my back, my shoulders, my legs and my bottom. All the time those blows rained down on me, words such as 'evil', 'bad' and 'discipline' spewed out of her mouth. The pain was so intense I felt hot tears spurt from my eyes and Davie gasped with fear, but still she shouted at me and beat me with that strap.

When she finally stopped I was shaking convulsively, and my back and legs were burning with the unaccustomed pain. Gloria had often swiped me but no one had ever hurt me like that before and I was rigid with shock and fear. Out of the corner of my eye I saw that Neville seemed to be enjoying watching my punishment; the tip of his tongue licked his wet, fleshy lips.

'Now get in there and do as you are told,' Sister Freda shouted. She shoved me fiercely into the room, Davie stumbled after me and the door slammed shut.

Only two days before, John, Davie and I had been together at home. It only took two days at Sacre Coeur to make me shake with fear and trepidation. And now we had to work for this loathsome man; I don't know how but I could already sense that Neville was a threat to us both.

I forced myself to focus on the room. When I did, I saw about twenty terrified chickens flapping their wings and trying to escape from Neville's huge hands. He sniggered with glee as they clucked in panic, beat their wings, jumped on any surface they could find; they were climbing over each other as they tried to get away and pecking frantically at his fingers, but there was no escaping Neville.

'Watch this, boys,' he said with a wide grin that contained a strange level of excitement but no humour, and to our horror he picked up a chicken and threw it on the floor so hard that we heard the crack of tiny bones breaking in its wing. His foot came down on it. 'This one's for the nuns' table so we mustn't hurt it too much,' he said with a smirk. 'Can't have its nice white flesh bruised now, can we? Stops it tasting nice, that does.'

He picked up a small gleaming axe and with one fast whack brought it down sharply on the chicken's neck. Its head rolled off but its eyes, which only a split second earlier had registered its terror, remained open. Davie gave a little whimper and turned his face away towards me.

Neville lifted his foot off the chicken and, to our increasing horror, the headless creature stood up, raised its wings and ran around the room, flapping its death throes as it spurted hot, bright-red blood on the floor, on us and on the other terrified chickens. We watched in disgust and macabre fascination, wondering how it could be so obviously dead and yet apparently so alive. Finally it slowed down and Neville picked it up and hung it on one of a line of hooks on the wall, with the blood still dripping from its neck. He repeated this brutal act many more times, laughing and obviously relishing the remaining chickens' escalating distress and our stricken faces.

'What's the fuss about anyhow? You eat the bloody things, don't you? What do you think happens? Think they lie down and die quietly next to the pot?' He roared with laughter at what he thought was his hilarious joke.

'I want those heads picked up and put in there,' he said, pointing to a box. 'And if they are still on the floor when I come back, do you know what I'm going to do, Robbie?'

Speechlessly I shook my head.

'I'll hang you up with the chickens right on that special peg,' he said, still with that wide grin on his face. 'See it? It's higher than the others. I had it made for little boys just like you.' He held the axe against my face, grazing the skin ever so slightly. It was covered in blood-soaked feathers and silvery strands of chicken gore. I could feel it and smell it. I was determined not to give him the satisfaction of seeing me rub my cheek clean.

'So if you don't fancy hanging there, get moving – both of you.' His hand patted me on the bottom and lingered there, its fingers prodding into my flesh. 'I've got to go to the kitchen. Be back soon. So don't go anywhere.' Laughing that sinister laugh, he opened the door and walked through it.

When it closed I put my ear to it and tried to hear his footsteps fading. Surely we could get out of here, find John and escape? We could live on the beach. We could be castaways again, couldn't we?

I tried the door. It was locked. I wanted to throw myself against it, beat it with my fists, kick it with my feet, scream out my frustration, but I did none of those things. Instead, as instructed, I picked up the blood-soaked chickens' heads and put them into the box.

I averted my eyes from the pitiful hanging corpses. I tried not to look at my little brother to prevent his fear transmitting itself to me. I also tried to ignore the terror of the remaining chickens. They might not have been the most intelligent of creatures, but they certainly seemed to know that they were about to suffer a horrible end.

I felt tears starting to leak out and leant against the locked door in despair. The sound of Neville's advancing footfalls made me spring away from it, though, and I hurriedly wiped away the moisture under my eyes. I didn't want him to see any signs of weakness.

'Now I've got another nice little job for you two namby-pambies,' he said as soon as he entered. 'You're going to pull all those feathers out. See here?' He pointed to a deep tin bath. 'That gets filled with nearly boiling hot water from the geyser.' I glanced at the old-fashioned geyser that rumbled and steamed away in the corner. Next to it was a huge enamel jug that I assumed was used to carry the hot water.

'Robbie, you can help me fill the bath and then in go the chickens; just for a couple of minutes, mind – can't have them getting cooked!' He laughed at the picture that this thought conjured up in his head, then went on to explain that boiling water loosened the feathers and would make Davie's and my job easier.

He threw the first couple of chickens in once the bath was three-quarters filled, and then scooped them out with a large ladle after a few minutes.

'This is how it's done. Just hold these feathers tight at the bottom and pull them quickly and out they come. Easy job, that is.' He looked up at me with a broad, satisfied smirk on his face.

'What are you waiting for? Get started,' he told us and placed a steaming hot, wet bird in my arms.

The smell was terrible, like wet pillows. I sat on the floor feeling sicker and sicker as each handful of feathers I pulled out exposed more puckered, pallid skin beneath. My little brother's face was screwed up and his mouth drooped but he silently copied what I was doing. Feathers stuck to our clothes, in our hair and all over our hands. I could even feel them trying to go up my nose as I breathed in.

All the time I sat on the floor pulling feathers out of the dead chickens, seeing the steam rise from the tin bath, hearing the splash as yet another bird was thrown in, I was aware of Neville's eyes watching us.

He's waiting for us to cry, I thought, but I'm not going to. I mustn't and I didn't.

In the playground later, I found Nicolas and asked him about Neville.

'Oh no, have you been sent to the chicken-killing room?' he asked sympathetically. 'You're right to be wary of Neville.'

He told us that Neville had been born on Jersey and brought to Sacre Coeur when still only a few days old. Rumours amongst the boys said that he was such an ugly baby that when his mother first set eyes on him she was so overcome with horror that she bribed the midwife to keep his birth a secret. She hid him from sight and told friends and relatives he had been stillborn. Then, in the darkness of the night, she left him at the gates of Sacre Coeur.

During the time he lived there, neither the baby Neville nor the teenage one had sufficiently moved the heart of any visitors for him to be invited to leave the orphanage and live in a new home. Over the years that he had been cared for by the nuns he had grown into a man large in stature and low in intellect, and he had learnt the skills of manipulation and obsequiousness. When Neville reached the age when other boys were normally left to fend for themselves, the nuns, believing in his loyalty and fearing for his ability to cope with the reality of the world outside, decided to allow him to stay. After all, with his limited intelligence, his squat overweight body and his face that repelled even the most generous of spirits, it was unlikely that he would ever gain employment. But to the nuns he was an asset – young, strong and, with them, biddable. As long as he was fed and clothed he demanded no wages. He needed no money, for everything he wanted was at Sacre Coeur.

Neville was placed in charge of the chicken sheds. He made sure the eggs were collected and put into boxes ready to be sold. He supervised the cleaning of the deep litter barns and organised the killing of the chickens. Scrawny birds, past their egg-laying days, were destined for our greasy stews and the young tender plump birds were destined for the nuns' table.

Neville liked looking after the chickens for it gave him the opportunity to indulge all three of his main interests: eating copious amounts of food, inflicting pain on small creatures and molesting little boys.

I listened to the story with a chill in my bones, and hoped fervently that I would never be sent back to the chicken-killing rooms to work with him again.

That night in bed I curled up as tightly as I could. I could still hear Davie's muffled sobs but this time I couldn't bring myself to go to him. I didn't want to be a big brother; I wanted John back so he could be mine.

My legs and back still smarted from the beating Sister Freda had given me, and when I closed my eyes an army of headless chickens, their wings flapping and their necks splattering thick arcs of blood, came marching towards me.

'Please, Stanley,' I whispered into my pillow. 'Please, please get better soon and come and get us all.'

Chapter Thirteen

On our fourth day at Sacre Coeur, which was a Monday, I was taken to a new school, one where all the orphans aged five to eleven went. Every morning after our hastily consumed breakfast the nuns, smiling graciously at passers-by, marched us in a crocodile from Sacre Coeur to the school gates.

Davie had to stay behind at the orphanage. At not quite four he was too young for school. A young nun called Sister Claire, who had a strong French accent, was evidently in charge of the little ones. 'Don't worry, Robbie,' she said, holding Davie's hand. 'They'll be all right with me. I've got charge of the young ones today.' I noticed then that she had a row of freckles across her nose and her smile reached her eyes. I was pleased that it was her who would be looking after Davie.

The very first day at my new school, I knew I wasn't going to like it. There was no friendly Miss Darby who knelt down to my height when she had something important to say to me, smiled reassuringly when I tried to give the right answer to a question and heaped praise on me when I succeeded. At this school the teacher in charge of the infants was an overweight, harassed woman who didn't seem to like small boys, especially orphaned and abandoned ones.

With my Sacre Coeur uniform and hair clipped almost to my scalp, I was keenly aware of looking different from the others in the classroom. There was no other boy from the orphanage in my class and my classmates showed little interest in becoming my friend. For a few moments when I first went in many curious eyes looked me up and down, then they noted my outward differences and turned away.

To add to my discomfort was the embarrassment of yet again having lunch boxes sent in by a charitable organisation. At this school, we charity cases were put in a separate room to eat instead of sitting with the other children who had brought in home-made lunch boxes. If our uniforms had already marked us out as different, being fed separately made it look as though we were being deliberately segregated.

Sometimes I heard the other children mutter the word 'Bastard!' and I'd scurry along the corridor with my head down. I knew that being a bastard was worse than being an orphan. I also knew that I was not going to find it easy to make new friends there but I didn't fully understand why.

Every morning before school I was put to work with Nicolas, sweeping the huge tiled hall. That took us almost an hour before breakfast. At four o'clock, when the school bell rang we all trooped back to Sacre Coeur for more chores before supper at five fifteen. The days fell into a pattern and Davie and I began to find out what was expected of us. Then, on the Friday morning a week after our arrival, there was a new development.

'Tonight after supper you're both to come for your baths,' Sister Freda told us. 'You pick up your washbag and come to the bath area, and no dawdling mind.'

Nicolas explained to me that half the boys bathed one week and the other half the following one. 'Bad luck,' he said. 'This week is the one where Sister Bernadette and Sister Freda are there. They're the worst.'

'What do you mean?' I asked, puzzled by his remark and the short harsh laugh that accompanied it.

'They like to make sure you are really clean everywhere,' Nicolas replied, then he turned away and I knew that was all he would tell me.

The old nun on supper duty told everyone who was going for a bath to leave first. Davie and I followed a stream of boys. Up the stairs we went until we came to a large room that had been converted into five oblong cubicles using sheets of chipboard. Two doors were fitted to each one and there were benches outside.

Two boys I didn't know, Davie and I were called through.

'Take all your clothes off,' instructed Sister Claire, the French nun who looked after Davie while I was at school. She turned her face away modestly to avoid seeing our naked bodies.

'Hang your trousers and jumpers on those pegs above your heads and throw your dirty socks and underwear into the boxes by your feet. When you come out I'll give you each clean ones.'

We were told to sit on some wooden benches in the passage outside. The clean underwear and socks were waiting in baskets beneath it. Davie was still too young to be self-conscious but the other two boys, who were roughly my age, and I tried to hide our shrivelled little penises from view. We crouched over like little old men, our arms folded low down on our chests. We were shivering with the cold and goose bumps rose on our arms as we waited. Getting into a bath full of hot water suddenly seemed an attractive proposition. Two boys came out of the tiny bathroom we were waiting to enter, both wearing dripping-wet, baggy grey underpants that they pulled off and quickly passed to Davie and me.

'You're next,' they told us. 'You have to put these on before you go in there.'

We looked at them in amazement.

'The nuns mustn't see us without our clothes. It's a mortal sin for a woman to look at a naked boy's body,' the older boy explained patiently.

I shrugged my shoulders. It seemed pretty stupid to me but I still pulled on my sodden pair and Davie wriggled into his ones that were far too big for him. We padded over to the cubicle door and went in cautiously.

Inside we saw a small white enamel bath and a chair, set in a windowless, whitewashed cupboard of a room. I was dismayed to see that Sister Bernadette was waiting for us because all Nicolas's warnings about her rang in my ears.

'Climb in, both of you,' she instructed. 'Take your soap and flannel and wash yourselves everywhere, except' – she paused to give even greater impact to her words of warning – 'you are not to put your hands inside your pants. Do you understand me?'

I stared, wondering if I had heard her correctly. It sounded a strange command but I tried to hide my thoughts and simply said, 'Yes, Sister,' for I knew that to question her orders was to invite her wrath – something I certainly didn't want to witness.

The bathwater already looked scummy. At least four other bodies that had not seen soap and water for two weeks had been immersed in it already. Still, we were used to shared bathwater so, not paying much heed, Davie and I levered ourselves in.

I turned my eyes away from Sister Bernadette, not because of modesty but because her penetrating gaze made me feel uncomfortable. I picked up my soap and flannel and started washing myself. I rubbed the flannel under my arms and across my chest, I soaped the back of my neck and behind my ears, then I closed my eyes and ducked under the water to wash my hair.

'Finished,' I thought to myself as I shook the drops from my head and stood up to step out.

'Wherever do you think you're going?' she asked. 'You're not finished yet. Pass me your flannel and soap and your brother's as well. Now lean back and put your hand on the sides and keep perfectly still. We have got to get you clean everywhere.'

She bent forward and placed one podgy hand firmly on my chest. The other hand grasped the flannel and slid it quickly under those underpants. I felt the rub of the cloth against my penis as her strong fingers tugged my foreskin up and down harder and harder.

'Clean everywhere is what you have to be,' her voice chanted in my ear. 'No touching yourselves there. You touch yourself and God will know and you will go straight to Hell. Do you understand?'

My eyes were watering. The smarting of my penis coupled with an awakening shame took my voice away. I could only whisper, 'Yes, Sister,' even though I didn't really understand what she meant. How could I avoid touching myself there? I held it when I peed, didn't I? She hadn't said anything about that. Would that make me go to Hell?

Nicolas told me later that it was not the actual touching of my penis that was the sin but if I enjoyed it. Whatever the nuns said, he told me that when I got older I would enjoy holding and touching my penis. He said it would also feel good when I moved my hand up and down.

But that day in the bath, I only knew that it hurt. It hurt a lot.

Chapter Fourteen

On our second Saturday, as soon as we had eaten our breakfast, once again Sister Freda appeared to escort us to Neville's lair.

'Neville told me how hard you both worked last Saturday,' she told us grudgingly, 'and said he wanted you to help him again.'

My heart sank. I had hoped and hoped all week that we wouldn't have to return to his outhouse, but he had forestalled us.

When we arrived, we saw that Neville had done something different with the chickens. Instead of bringing them from the deep litter barns in boxes and releasing them in the killing shed, he had caught the birds three at a time, tied their legs together, carried them across the few yards from the barn and thrown them onto the flagstone floor. There they lay in pitiful feathered heaps, feebly trying to break free and escape. He smirked at the birds' plight but it was clear that his fun was far from over.

He picked them up, held them out at arm's length and laughed out loud as they beat their wings and contorted their bodies, trying to reach their tormentor's hands and peck them.

'Naughty, naughty!' he said as he hung them up by their bound feet onto the pegs in squirming, clucking bunches. 'Mustn't be nasty to Neville.' He whispered to us: 'Now I've got a new job for you, Robbie. See this bowl?'

I nodded suspiciously.

'That's to catch the blood when I cut their throats. The nuns want it for the gardens. Say it's good for the flowers. So catch every drop and no blood on the floor. OK?'

He thrust the bowl into my unwilling hands, went up to the feathery mass, caught one chicken's head in his hand and with the other hand sliced its throat so that the head hung by a thread and blood spurted out in fat, dark-red globs. Neville quickly pulled me in front of him, holding me tightly against his body. He lifted my arms and positioned the bowl under the bird.

The blood dripped in. I smelled its ripe, metallic odour and, combined with the stale musky stench of Neville's body, it nauseated me. I was only five and I just couldn't comprehend that there was something about the combination of the smell of blood and the fear and panic of the helpless creatures that thrilled Neville, but I was aware that they did. I could feel a peculiar sense of pleasure and enjoyment in his quickened breath that raised the hairs on the back of my neck; the rising heat of him so close to me seemed to penetrate right through my jumper. When I wriggled free and turned round I saw the tip of his tongue licking the edges of his fleshy mouth in a way that was quite repulsive. He always seemed to do this when he was excited, I noticed.

One after another he systematically slit the throats of those poor chickens. He chuckled with delight as they twisted and turned in their slow, bloody death throes. Once the first batch of chickens was still, he severed their heads with a quick flick of his hunting knife and allowed them to drop to the floor.

'Davie, you're to pick up the heads. I know it was Robbie did it last week so it's your turn this time.'

Davie shook his head defiantly.

As he slowly comprehended that a three-year-old boy was challenging his orders, a sudden look of delight spread across Neville's ugly features. Out of his pocket he took a length of thick twine. He caught both Davie's hands in one of his and, using his other hand and his teeth, he quickly tied them together. I stood rooted to the spot with fear.

'I warned you what happens to little boys who say the word "no" to me.' He picked Davie up by his knotted wrists and hung him from a free peg set between the dead chickens on one side and the last untouched bunch of flapping, living ones on the other. Neville sliced one of their throats and pulled it so it dripped blood close to Davie's face.

'Your turn next!' he said. Davie's face turned chalky white, except for two spots that flamed bright red on his cheeks. His eyes fluttered shut, and his body hung limply.

I guessed he must have fainted. What could I do to help him? There's no way I could fight Neville – I knew that.

'Now, Robbie, your little brother is going to have to stay there unless you do something for me. Do you know what I want you to do?'

I shook my head. I wanted to beg him to let Davie down. I was so scared for him. He wasn't making a sound. But I already knew that begging Neville would just make it worse. 'Don't cry, Davie,' I silently pleaded. 'Don't scream, or yell. If you stay still he'll get fed up.' I looked at the knife in Neville's hand and shivered. Would Davie suffer the same terrible fate as the chickens? With mounting horror I watched as Neville snaked his hand out towards Davie. It slid up his little legs and disappeared under his pants.

'Come here, Robbie,' Neville said in a voice I had not heard before. 'Do you want me to let your brother down or do you want to go up alongside him?'

I tried desperately not to show the fear that gnawed inside of me. 'Let him down, please,' I whispered, my voice catching in my throat.

'And you'll do anything I ask? 'Cos if you don't, it will be worse for him.'

Pee was running down Davie's legs. I felt his terror and I knew that's what had paralysed him. He hadn't fainted; he was just scared to death.

'Yes,' I replied.

Neville lifted Davie down but left his wrists tied and roughly propped him against the wall. Davie slumped forward.

Neville lowered his huge frame onto a chair. He pulled me towards him until I was standing between his legs, then he unfastened the buttons of his trousers and lowered them slightly. He lifted his penis out of his grubby underpants. I had never seen a man's one before, not even Stanley's. It didn't look as big as I had thought it would. John had told me that when you were a man they grew very big, like a banana. Neville's was just poking out from under rolls of fat and lay limply on the top of his white thigh.

He grasped my small hand and wrapped my fingers around his penis.

'Move your hand up and down,' he instructed.

I did.

I couldn't look at him or at Davie so I looked somewhere just over his shoulder. I didn't want to look into his face, didn't want to see those fleshy lips, which I somehow knew were being wetly caressed by his tongue. Neither did I want to listen to his heavy breathing, but I could feel each hot, fetid breath blowing on my cheek. Nor did I want to feel that warm, slimy, sticky substance that trickled into my hand and dripped through my fingers.

'Better wash them before you pluck those chickens,' was all he said when he pushed me away.

He untied my brother's hands. They were red where the rope had cut into his flesh.

As if nothing had happened, Neville filled the tin bath with boiling water and started to throw the chicken carcasses into it.

Without a look or a word passing between us, Davie and I began to pluck the chickens. Davie never disobeyed Neville again.

From being my favourite day, the one I looked forward to all week, the day all three of us went to the beach or the park, the day John was with us, a day full of laughter and fun, Saturday now became the day I dreaded the most. For everything that was loathsome and everything that was corrupt was conjured up in one word: Neville. And every Saturday Davie and I were sent to work with him.

I wondered whether he spent all week preparing himself for our visit. Did he lick those fleshy lips in anticipation of our tears? Did he plan the first time he fondled us, when he rubbed his large, flabby body against our small firm ones and yanked his penis up and down in front of us? Was that the highlight of his week?

Maybe it was. Subconsciously, over time, we began to fight back. Not straight away, because it took some months for us to gain enough inner strength, but eventually we did. Eventually Davie stopped crying and I stopped shaking. Instead we stared back at him and wiped all evidence of emotion and feeling from our faces. That way, we felt, he hadn't won. That way we could spoil at least some of his disgusting fun.

Chapter Fifteen

When I look back at that time some memories are so sharp and clear that I can still feel the sadness that was the essence of my five-year-old self. Others are like an old photograph left partially forgotten at the back of a wallet or the bottom of a drawer. Time has faded it, creases mar its surface and at first glance the people from yesterday, depicted in it, are almost unrecognisable. But we know that should we allow our defences to weaken, the image will become sharper and the features familiar until we are once again face to face with the horrors of our past.

Those pictures in my head of those first months at Sacre Coeur are like those old black-and-white photographs, for I can only remember dark, dull days. It's as though my little-boy misery has sucked all the colour from my early memories of Sacre Coeur. I'm sure that the sun must have shone on our Channel Island; it was spring when we went there, but I don't remember one single ray of its warmth. I remember other things though. The austerity, the daily rituals and the smell of burning porridge that greeted us each morning. Queuing outside the dining room before every mealtime for our hands and necks to be inspected; knowing we would go hungry should any dirt be found.

Having to stand and recite grace before and after meals. The morning mass; the evening mass, when we were so tired that all we could think about was sleep. The smell of incense, the click of rosaries, the huge statues of a man whose heart was exposed, eyes rolled up in agony and thorns covering his head, appearing to beckon us with his bloodstained hands. And the blessed Mother Mary who was said to love little children – but not the ones at Sacre Coeur, we were convinced.

Over time we learnt if not to like, then at least to tolerate the institutionalised food. At breakfast we had lumpy, thin, tasteless porridge made with water. At first I yearned for something sweet to flavour it – syrup and rich, creamy Jersey milk – but knowing neither was forthcoming, gradually I learnt to eat it with salt. The remainder of our breakfast was two slices of coarse, wheaten bread and dripping. Once a month and on holy days, boiled eggs were put in front of us, but all the other eggs produced by the laying hens in the deep litter barns were either served at the nuns' table or sold to local shop-keepers.

The most common main meal of the day was a greasy stew that consisted of whatever vegetables were in season and chicken complete with skin and bones. Those plucked, pallid birds were carried from Neville's outhouse and piled up on the wooden kitchen table. Each one was hastily chopped into six portions, thrown into a large pot along with some vegetables and potatoes and there it bubbled, filling the air with unappetising aromas.

At first, when I saw how the grease floated out of the skin to stain the surface with pale yellow streaks, I looked at it with disgust. When the old nun ladled it out onto my plate at dinner-time I tried not to think of the terrified creatures that Neville had killed, or how I had had to pluck them, or what Neville made me do to him in the chicken killing room. Instead I chewed, swallowed, spat out bones, licked my lips and wiped my plate clean. Hunger has a knack of making the most terrible food palatable, and with no between-meal snacks hunger was something I got used to.

My sixth birthday came and went without comment except that I was given another chore to do: instead of just sweeping the huge entrance hall Nicolas and I had to wash and polish it every morning as well.

A few weeks later the summer holidays started. That year, unlike the previous one, there was no excitement; no big brother coming home saying 'That's it for six weeks.' No beach that we could go to and swim and play 'Castaways'. No swings in the park and no freedom. Instead we faced six weeks of being under the rigorous discipline of the nuns who, with their belief that the Devil finds work for idle hands, made doubly sure that mine were very, very busy.

After I had helped Nicolas clean the hall we had breakfast and then attended mass from Monday through to Friday. After mass, I was sent to work in the laundry, a huge noisy room with a damp, steamy smell, along with Marc, a ginger-haired boy about two years older than me.

The walls were lined with deep, white rectangular sinks. Heavy ridged washboards used for scrubbing lay on the wooden draining boards and mangles with basins placed underneath them stood in a corner. In the centre of the room were the gas burners where huge pans of water bubbled away. In them we threw grubby white bedding and towels to which we added soap powder and a small amount of bleach. About an hour later a pair of older boys used giant wooden tongs to remove the boiling-hot washing and dump it into baskets. Our task was to drag these away and rinse the washing before hanging it out to dry. Over our heads were wooden drying racks that hung from the ceiling and a heavy pulley enabling them to be raised and lowered.

The first task I was given was to separate dirty socks from underpants, jumpers from shirts, pyjamas from day clothes. Once they were piled in separate stacks I, and several other boys of a similar age, filled the sinks with soapy water, cold for the wool and warm for everything else. We propped up the metal and wooden ridged boards beside them and rubbed and rubbed until even the most stubborn stains had been removed.

They were then rinsed in another sink filled with cold water: no point wasting hot water on clean clothes, the nuns told us, thus making the task of rinsing take twice as long. Once one sink-load of washing had been completed we would try our best to wring it out, but our hands were too small to be of much use. We pulled out bundles of wet clothes and sheets, placed them in the wicker baskets and trailed them across the floor to be put through the mangles. We fed those dripping wet clothes, sheets and towels through the heavy roller, then grasped the handle with both hands and turned it over and over until, after a number of times through the mangle, the washing was merely damp.

Back in our wicker baskets it went, to be dragged over to the racks. Bigger boys pulled them down for us to hang everything up to dry.

We repeated that exercise again and again until our backs and arms ached unbearably by the end of the day. My hands were red and sore. It was hard, heavy work. Our days were ruled by the ringing of the bell announcing either a mealtime or mass.

Marc and I used to whisper to each other when we weren't being watched – rude comments about the nuns, and the kind of chatter that little boys enjoy. Making a new friend was the only bonus to working there.

I spent the entire summer indoors in that laundry. The job was so relentless I almost looked forward to going back to school. That, I thought, would be an easier option. But I was wrong.

Chapter Sixteen

There were other boys like Davie and me who had living parents but for one reason or another had been placed in the orphanage. Sometimes one parent had died, leaving the other unable to cope. Or a husband had gone to England to work, leaving behind a family with no money and only the promise of a cheque that never came. Then there were the children the nuns considered the worst: children whose mothers had never been married to their father – usually because as soon as the man in question was told of the pregnancy he promptly disappeared off the island. Sometimes it was the gossip and turned heads in our small community or the financial struggle to bring up a child alone that was too much; other times it was the appearance of a new man who didn't want another man's child giving a constant reminder of previous relationships. Whatever it was, all these children ended up in the orphanage.

There were many explanations and just as many excuses. Stories would be told by excited little boys of the promises their grandmother, mother, elder brother, even sometimes their out-of-work father had made to them. The promise was that the moment a house or a job was found, a pay packet arrived from England or the new man discovered he really liked children, then they would be going home. But however many promises weren't kept, however many little boys' hearts were broken and however many tears fell when their dreams turned into shattered hopes, the one thing that all those boys had that Davie and I hadn't were relatives who came to visit.

I watched with longing as other boys chatted with family members, who promised them that soon they would be leaving and going home. Each time I saw the short-lived happiness on those boys' faces, I yearned to see someone walk through those doors looking for me.

Surely Stanley must be better now? Surely soon he and Gloria would come for us? Every time I saw a bed suddenly become empty, I knew that little boy had gone somewhere better. Sometimes a relative had been able to meet their promise; other times we knew they had been adopted and taken to a new home.

Occasionally there were visiting days when other people came to see us as well, and they were referred to by the nuns as 'visitors'. We all knew why they were there – because they wanted a child of their own. Mostly it was couples that came, the woman roughly Gloria's age, though there the similarity ended. Whereas Gloria favoured thick make-up, colour-enhanced long hair and tight-fitting clothes, these women had pale faces unadorned with make-up, demure pastel jumpers over pleated skirts that covered their knees, and shiny hair that they wore in a simple pageboy style.

Those couples usually walked straight past us boys to the area where the small children and toddlers were. There they stopped, knelt down and made baby-talk noises. We grinned at each other with bravado to show we didn't care that they had no interest in us. It meant we were big boys, didn't it? We had already learnt that to express a wish even to ourselves was to court disappointment.

To begin with, I did worry that so many of the couples seemed to want to adopt babies. What if Denise was adopted? How would we ever find her again? Whenever I got a chance, I would try to peer through to the babies' section but I never caught so much as a glimpse of her. But as time went on, I'm ashamed to say that the memory of Denise faded.

Other 'visitors' came to the dining room after grace had been said. They sat at a table with little boys who looked bewildered at the attention. The women would wipe crumbs off sticky cheeks, brush silky strands of hair back from solemn little faces and smile sweetly into pleading eyes. The men would ruffle the hair on an upturned head, but say very little.

We were never told which boy had been picked. It was not until about a week later that his empty bed told us who had been the lucky one that time. 'He's been adopted,' Nicolas always said knowingly, with a wistful look on his face.

I would try to imagine what those boys' lives would become. Would they be wearing new clothes perhaps knitted and sewn from the patterns in *Woman's Weekly*, riding a shiny new bicycle and playing with their very own puppy?

We always knew that we would never see that boy again; the happiness of the outside world would swallow him up.

Sometimes the visitors were older couples who had lost a son in the war and wanted to give a home to a deserving orphaned boy. With them it was always the men who asked the questions, such as which school subject was their favourite and what hobbies did they have.

The boy always replied as he had been instructed: 'I like reading, sir, but I don't have a great deal of time for it as I have a lot of schoolwork to do each night' – omitting from his answer the fact that Sacre Coeur's routine left little time for hobbies and that the only reading material allowed was religious books.

The next question was nearly always the same: 'What do want to do when you leave school?' No boy hopeful of adoption ever gave the truthful answer: 'Don't care, as long as I get out of here.' Instead they gave the acceptable one: 'I would like to go to university, sir, and study ...' It was only the desired subject that changed from one boy to the next.

Every time a new visitor arrived, each child old enough to understand hoped that this time they were going to be the one; the one who was going to be chosen to live in a big house, eat tasty, home-cooked food and sleep between crisp, clean sheets in their own bedroom.

The visitors I didn't like were the single men, the ones who told us they wanted to be an uncle. Mainly in their thirties and forties, they were well-dressed, usually in blazers and flannels. With their sleeked-back hair and tanned faces, even to my untrained eyes they looked wealthy. White teeth flashed under waxed moustaches as they fussed over little boys aged between five and nine years old. I watched the happy faces of those boys, saw their hopeful expressions and then, over the following days, watched their excited anticipation. In these cases we always guessed which boy had been chosen. It was the one they had sat on their knee, the one to whom they had surreptitiously given a bar of chocolate, the one they had hugged when leaving.

Every weekend, I worried about what would happen if the nuns had not told the visitors that Denise, Davie and I already had a mother and father. Had they explained that we were only there because Stanley was sick? When those visitors who wanted a little boy came, I refused to put on a happy face. I lowered my head or, if possible, hid in a corner and tried to keep Davie at my side and as quiet as possible. From there, I silently watched the comings and goings.

Sometimes there was a different type of visitor; the nuns called them the 'searchers'. Most of them were tired-looking Frenchmen and women whose lined faces and stooped shoulders gave off a mixture of sorrow and faint hope. I didn't understand why that sadness clung to them, but I recognised it. The nuns hovered around these people; nuns whom I had never seen show any compassion laid comforting hands on arms and spoke softly. They stood close, trying to form a gentle barrier against hurt. The searchers always seemed to be looking for someone they had once known and it was always the older boys they approached.

'Do you know the name of your papa, your mamma?' they would ask hopefully. 'Do you know where you came from?' As bewildered boys shook their heads, disappointment blazed briefly in the searchers' eyes.

Sometimes those people were elderly and spoke with American accents. They puzzled me, those sad people, and as a child I wondered if it was their grandchildren they were looking for. It was not until I was an adult that I worked it out.

During the German occupation of Europe underground organisations helped to hide Jewish children, in attics and cellars or in the middle of someone else's family in deserted country areas, anywhere they might be safe. They were known as the 'hidden children of Europe'. Parents said their goodbyes in the hope but without any belief that one day they would be reunited, before turning to face their own fates.

As the war spread across Europe and the Nazis' relentless purge of Jews stretched its tentacles to every corner of each country they occupied, friends became foes, children were found, fair-haired women were exposed as Jewesses and the records of the hidden children were destroyed for their own protection.

For years after the war ended there was hope that there were more of those 'hidden children' surviving somewhere. Not one orphanage in Europe was left unvisited by relatives hoping that there was just one more member of their family left. I wonder now if those searchers ever found a child who had been hidden safely as a baby. I certainly hope so.

Chapter Seventeen

As the summer faded and the evenings drew in, draughts crawled under windows and doors, pinched fingers and sent shivers up spines; our breath misted windows as we peered out on dark frosty mornings.

That winter, I learnt the reality of the word cold.

Christmas came. Our morning routine was the same except that after breakfast we had an even longer mass than usual. Before lunch we were taken to a room where toys were stacked. They were the discarded, forgotten teddy bears, trains and model cars of children who had outgrown them so their parents had donated them to the orphanage.

'Choose one each,' Sister Bernadette told us. 'And no pushing, mind.'

I found a packet of crayons and took those. Davie picked up a battered Dinky car with only a hint of paint left on it. I looked in vain to see if there was an easel and thought longingly of the one Stanley had given me the previous Christmas. Where was it now, I wondered.

The New Year was rung in, the days eventually started to grow warmer and I woke up one morning to the realisation that a whole year had passed since I'd walked through the doors of Sacre Coeur. It was then that I began to panic because my family were becoming blurred images. All of a sudden, instead of the clear picture that I always used to be able to see in my head, it was becoming fuzzy. 'What will happen if they don't come soon?' I worried, anxious that I wouldn't recognise them.

Sometimes I felt with despair that not only had I lost John but, in a different way, I'd lost Davie as well. My plump, chatty little brother with his ever-ready smile and cheerful nature had disappeared, leaving in his place a thinner, more solemn child, who spoke rarely and smiled even less. He was the last contact with my family and my only barrier against loneliness and, in desperation, I would try everything in my power to coax a smile from him.

'Come on, Davie,' I said time after time. 'Look, I'll draw you a picture, make you a paper aeroplane or tell you about my day at school.' Not the really bleeding awful times I had there, I won't tell you about them – I'll try and find the nice bits for you. 'Just smile for me, Davie. Please smile at me.' But he never did.

I would take paper and a crayon out of my school satchel. 'Let me draw you a picture of ...' and I would list all the things he had asked me to draw for him in the past – animals, cars, boats – but he would just knock my hand to one side. 'Don't want,' he said and looked away from me as though by needing his attention I had become his enemy. 'Don't want,' he repeated – two words that had become his favourite ones, with 'no' coming a close second.

'Want John,' he said when he knew only I could hear him. And as those words left his mouth, tears filled his eyes and dribbled down his cheeks; and this time his tears filled me not with pity but with rage. For every silver drop that stained his cheeks only served to remind me just how much I also missed my eldest brother. His not being there was a constant ache that never left me. In bed, when they thought I was asleep, I talked to John, asked his advice, and if I imagined hard enough I could sometimes believe that I heard a reply. Over those first weeks in Sacre Coeur, he promised me that we would all be together again. And each night I asked him when. And he answered with the same repeated word: soon. On hearing it, I was reassured and fell asleep comforted by those words.

When I saw Davie's drooping mouth and the tears in his eyes that were fearfully gulped down when he saw the nuns, I started to feel the beginnings of a dull resentment; a resentment that grew little by little, day by day, until I begrudged taking him to the toilet, sitting next to him in the dining room and listening to his muffled sobs at night.

His constant presence began to irritate me. The only time he was not with me was when I was at school, but when I turned seven in a few months's time I knew that was going to change. Davie was due to start at the Infants the same term that I was being transferred into the Juniors.

Davie had one friend there, the little boy called Jimmy whom I had seen pushed off the bench at our first evening mass, the boy whose mother had died in childbirth and whose father had gone to England to find work. They were the same age and even shared the same birthday. I rarely saw them talking to each other but they walked around everywhere together as though they were joined at the hip and I could feel they had a strong connection.

When Davie and Jimmy both turned four, there was no celebration to mark the day; instead they were told that as they were no longer babies they were old enough to have their own chores to do. So at five forty-five on the morning of their shared birthday they joined the orphanage's workforce. Their only presents were a duster and a tin of furniture polish, and even those only belonged to them for the first two hours of the day. When their work was finished these items had to be returned to the nuns.

That meant that instead of staying in the special room for babies and toddlers until breakfast time, Davie followed me out to the hall. He had been ordered to dust and polish the right-hand side of the staircase while Jimmy did the left. Nicolas and I already had the huge hall to clean, a task that took all our efforts to finish in time before breakfast. First it had to be swept, then mopped and rinsed. Water had to be used sparingly; we couldn't make it easier by throwing soapy buckets of water over the floor because it had to be dry enough for us to polish before we finished. Otherwise, if Sister Freda's sharp eyes found a dirty mark on its shiny surface, we had to do it all over again and miss our breakfast. So we rubbed and rubbed with those damp mops and then got out the block polisher. Each holding an end, we worked that polisher back and forth until sweat dripped from our brows and onto the floor.

Sister Freda usually supervised the cleaning duties with eyes that missed not even a speck of dirt, but one day I realised she had wandered off. Maybe she thought that all the months we had spent in those highly disciplined conditions had sufficiently cowed us that we wouldn't dare to misbehave.

Without her forbidding presence and watchful stern-ness, I felt a sense of freedom that I hadn't experienced since we had been thrown into the back of the black police van. I jumped on top of the block polisher and grinned wickedly at Nicolas.

'Go on, Nicolas – give me a push.'

He had been in the home much longer than me, and at first he gave me a mystified look, but as he caught my mood this was replaced by mischievous glee. He put his weight behind the polisher and shoved with all his might.

'Push harder,' I instructed.

He laughed, and suddenly we reverted back to being little boys instead of the frightened, small robots the nuns had tried to turn us into. Whooping with the unexpected feeling of exhilaration and sheer pleasure, we raced up and down the hall until I lost my balance and fell. The sight of me sprawled on the floor sent Nicolas into spasms of infectious laughter, making me giggle so much that I couldn't get up.

When they heard the unexpected sounds of merri-ment, Davie and Jimmy stopped what they were doing and leant over the banisters to see me rolling on the floor. For the first time since we had come through the wooden doors of the home, I heard Davie laugh out loud. And seeing my little brother laugh, my resentment of him vanished as quickly as it had come and I loved him unconditionally again.

With his little face uncustomarily flushed, Jimmy decided he wanted to join in the fun and clambered up on the top of the banister and sat astride it. With a whoop he slid down, waving his hands in the air as he gained speed, and came to an abrupt stop when he reached the next landing down.

'Come on, Davie. You can do that,' I called. He leant his little body over the banister and threw one leg over, sat confidently astride it and started his descent, laughing out loud with the freedom and excitement of this act of rebellion.

Unfortunately, little boys having fun can neither do it silently nor can they think ahead to the repercussions of being caught. At first we didn't see Sister Bernadette and Sister Freda running into the hall, clutching their leather straps in their hands with looks of outraged fury on their faces. Then simultaneously all four of us became aware of their presence. There was a sudden silence: us frozen with fear, the nuns transfixed by the sight of four boys having the audacity to have fun. It only took a few seconds for that spell to break. Sister Bernadette's head turned towards me, her eyes locked on mine and the viciousness in their depths made me recoil. Then she turned her gaze to the stairs.

Jimmy had managed to climb off the banister and huddle down out of sight on the first-floor landing where I could see his scared little face poking through the struts. But when I looked up and saw where Davie was, I went rigid with fear. He was a couple of steps higher, still astride the banister, and his hands were clutching at the rail, trying to stop himself from sliding any further down.

'What do you think you are doing?' she shouted, her face almost purple with anger. One hand swished the leather strap in the air while the other clutched her habit, lifting it to just above ankle length as she took the stairs at a run, ascending two at a time.

'Get off, Davie,' I screamed. 'Get down from there.'

I felt icy tremors creep under my skin making me shiver with fear. I saw the leather strap swinging in Sister Bernadette's hand and we all knew that we would be made to pay dearly for our few minutes of joyous abandon.

I wanted to run up those stairs. I wanted to beg the nun to leave Davie alone; he was only a baby and it was entirely my fault, I had started it. Please, I wanted to say, he's so scared, don't frighten him any more. But my own fear kept me rooted to the spot and as hard as I tried to call out again, no sounds would come from my throat.

But then it was too late. The Sister had reached him and from the hall below I had a clear view of what happened next. Beside herself with rage, she raised the strap and swished it in the air once then twice above the small, crouching form of my terrified baby brother. He tried to sit up and at the same time he raised a hand from the rail to protect his head.

I heard Davie scream; I heard her shout and knew that the leather belt was raised to strike. The piercing sound of his next scream was followed by a silence, then a dull thud; the thud of something soft and small falling onto the floor below. My hands went over my eyes, my feet refused to move and I knew what it was without seeing.

I knew it was my brother.

A scream finally burst from my constricted throat. Sister Freda caught my arm with one hand and the back of my jumper with the other to stop me rushing to Davie. 'Leave him alone,' she instructed, holding me tightly.

'Let me go, let me go!' I yelled and I wriggled and squirmed in her grasp, trying in vain to break away from her. In desperation I kicked her as hard as I could on the shin. Shocked at this assault, she let go and I tore away. I raced across to where the small crumpled form of my four-year-old brother was lying. He wasn't moving; he was so still I was convinced he was dead.

I heard the clatter of Sister Bernadette racing down the stairs. I heard her shout at Davie to get up and then with great clarity I saw her push him with her foot as though he was subhuman. I was screaming hysterically now. Sister Freda caught me and yanked me away from the immobile little body, just as I was about to touch it.

Other nuns, alarmed by the disturbance, came running from all directions to see what was causing this early-morning rumpus. One grabbed Nicolas and pinned him against the wall.

'Get that boot cupboard open,' Sister Bernadette shouted at no one in particular and they obeyed, as they always did. The door to that dark musty cupboard was opened and I saw Sister Bernadette's booted, black-stocking-clad foot start to push Davie's inert form towards it.

I shouted at her, using the same words she had so often shouted at me: 'You're evil, you are!' Then I screamed Davie's name over and over until a hand was clamped firmly across my mouth.

The other nuns helped Sister Bernadette to push Davie's inert body into the dark cupboard.

I needed more than anything else in my life to get to my brother and make them leave him alone.

'Jimmy, you can go in to breakfast now,' Sister Bernadette said coldly. She obviously hadn't seen him doing anything wrong. 'But take those two to the sheds.' She pointed at Nicolas and me. 'Let them think about their sins in there.'

We screamed and shouted. We were beyond reason, even beyond fear. It crossed my mind that if they could kill Davie and not seem to care, they could also kill us. Other nuns stepped forward and helped Sister Freda to drag us from the hall and down the corridors. We struggled and hollered every inch of the way and we lashed out with our feet and hands as the terror we felt for Davie was compounded by the fear we had for ourselves.

'You are wicked boys,' panted Sister Freda. 'So bad that even those godless parents of yours didn't want you. Don't think we don't know everything about you and your older brother. Evil children, that's what you are.'

I heard a bolt being drawn, doors being opened and the hand that was clamped across my mouth was removed. With a hard push I was propelled into the foul-smelling interior of the deep litter barns. Disturbed by the light of the open door, chickens flew off their perches and landed near my feet. Their feathers brushed against my legs. I thought of the way they always pecked at my hands when I lifted eggs out from under them.

Then my imagination ran riot and allowed other terrifying thoughts to enter my head. What if these chickens knew where their missing friends had been taken? What if they had found out that it was me who helped Neville to murder them? There were hundreds of them in that barn. What if they all attacked us? I visualised all those sharp beaks and the beady little eyes of all the angry revengeful hens and cockerels that were hidden in the dark and was gripped by an immense terror.

A trickle of pee started to run down my leg.

Whimpering with fear, I looked back at the door where Sister Bernadette stood watching us.

'No, Sister, please don't leave us here. I need to go and help Davie.'

Nicolas's voice echoed my pleas. 'No, don't, please, Sister. I'm sorry; we won't do it again.'

In answer she let a harsh, mocking laugh escape her lips.

'Think about your sins now,' I heard Sister Freda's malevolent voice saying behind her before Sister Bernadette swung the barn doors shut, leaving two terrified boys in the dark.

Over the stench of the chickens I could smell the sharp ammonia smell of my own urine; the smell of fear.

The light faded and the shadows lengthened then deepened until we were engulfed in darkness. We heard the rattle and scraping of the old metal bolt as it slid firmly into place and knew that our pleas had been in vain; she had locked us in.

Chapter Eighteen

All around us we could sense the undulating movements of the mass of chickens, hear their clucking and feel the whispery strokes of their feathers brushing against our bare legs. My teeth began to chatter with fear. My eyes smarted and ran as the stench of the chicken shit mixed with the smell of damp seeped into my nostrils. I closed my eyes as if to try and shut down all my senses, only to have a terrifying word enter my mind – rats.

No sooner did the thought enter my head than pictures of large rodents with yellow teeth, eyes that saw in the dark, and fat scaly tails followed. Those loathsome creatures sometimes dug their way into the barn and lurked in corners, hoping for a feast of eggs. Traps were set for them, feral cats were brought in to catch them, but I knew that was not always enough. My whole body trembled, waves of sickness rose and any thought I had had of being brave deserted me. I put my arms out and clung to Nicolas for support. I was just so frightened and utterly helpless.

I tried in vain to push aside the question that was repeating itself over and over in my head: 'What has happened to my little brother?' The memory of that soft thump as his body hit the floor echoed in my ears. I felt a sharp pain in my diaphragm as though giant fingers were pinching me there. My breath started to come in short, shallow bursts. Stars floated in front of my eyes, making me squeeze them shut even tighter. I wanted to block out the reality of our situation, the terrifying darkness and the image of Davie's helpless little form being pushed and kicked towards the boot cupboard.

Perhaps sensing my rising hysteria, it was Nicolas who pulled himself together first.

'Come on, Robbie. We have to find somewhere to sit. Open your eyes. We'll just stand here till our eyes get used to the dark and we can see more.'

I clung to his arm even tighter. I was too petrified to do as he asked.

'The chickens are just as scared of us, you know. But they haven't pecked you, have they?'

True enough, although the birds were bumping into me they seemed indifferent to us and, realising that, I gradually stopped trembling. I decided not to mention rats and let go of Nicolas's arm. I strained to see in the dim light that leaked in under the door and between the slats of the boarded-up windows. First I focused on Nicolas, and could just see that his usually confident and smiling face was pale, tear-streaked and very miserable. I tried to smile at him and received a watery smile in return and a light punch on my arm.

I looked down at the mass of chickens that swirled around us and was greatly relieved to see that their heads were bent as they searched for food in the straw and dirt.

Suddenly I thought of something that would help. 'Hey, Nicolas,' I whispered; I was worried that the chickens might attack me if I spoke out loud. 'Where are the light switches? They're always switched on when we collect the eggs.'

'It's no good,' he answered. 'The switch is on the outside. It's in a little box to keep it dry. I used to wonder why. Now I know.'

I felt a wave of despondency as that fragile hope was dashed. My thoughts returned to poor Davie lying so still on the floor. He was dead and it was all my fault because I'd encouraged him to fool around. My heart ached and fresh tears welled up in my eyes.

'Come on, Robbie, we have to find somewhere to sit down,' Nicolas repeated. 'We need to be against a wall. We don't want to meet up with the cockerels, do we?'

A vivid picture of those brightly plumed, strutting birds came into my head. I gave a little shudder when I remembered how, when I was collecting eggs, they had raised their wings and beat them in an angry warning because I had inadvertently stepped too close to them.

Crab-like, I inched sideways, my eyes darting everywhere, searching for signs of danger. I hit the wall and leant against it thankfully.

'How long will they leave us here?' I asked.

'Until they think we've learnt our lesson,' Nicolas replied. 'I know one boy before your time they kept in here for two days.'

'Where is he now?'

'He got transferred to the mental hospital.'

I went quiet then. If children outside Sacre Coeur's walls were frightened of the bogeyman coming to take them away, we were scared of the men in white coats who might take us in the middle of the night, put needles in our arms and shoot electricity into our brains. Some older boys had told us these stories, enjoying watching our eyes widen with fear.

'If the nuns say that you have been really bad because you are sick in the head, that's what happens to you,' a boy told me. I hoped that wasn't what had happened to Stanley.

I closed my eyes again; the morning's events had completely tired me out. A mixture of fear and hunger – we had not had breakfast – made my stomach churn. My throat was dry and scratchy, my nose was running, my head buzzed with images of Davie's still body and I wanted to go to the lavatory. I didn't want to pee my pants again. I could still smell my last pee over the stench of the chickens and the tops of my legs felt cold and itchy.

I wriggled, trying to get more comfortable. I needed to stay awake because I was scared of what the chickens might do if they saw I was asleep. But the effort of keeping my eyes open was too much; my head grew heavy, my eyelids drooped and I fell into an uneasy doze.

I was wakened by the sound of a bolt being drawn back. The doors opened and light flooded in. I could see the silhouette of a nun and a smaller figure and as they came closer I saw it was Sister Claire, the young French nun, accompanied by Marc, my friend from the laundry.

Nicolas jumped to his feet and I followed suit. We hoped that she was going to let us out, but she explained that she wasn't allowed to do that. 'I have brought you some breakfast and a jug of water,' she said. 'There's a pail here for you to use as a toilet.'

'When will they let us out?' I asked, with fresh tears sliding down my cheeks.

'Soon' she said softly. 'Listen, Robbie, Davie is in the sick bay. He's sleeping now, but he's going to be all right. So dry your eyes and stop worrying.' I was so relieved, I sobbed even harder.

She smiled kindly. 'Marc's going to collect some eggs so the lights will be on for a bit. There's nothing to be scared of in here. It's just horrid for you both, that's all.'

She turned and left. Somehow I sensed she didn't approve of us being locked in there and that thought gave me some comfort. Nicolas and I ripped open the bag she had put our breakfast in and gasped with pleasure. Everything in there must have come off the nuns' table. There were hard-boiled eggs, thick slices of fresh bread spread with real butter, chunks of yellow cheese and three apples: food we seldom saw or got to eat. She had also left a bottle of creamy milk.

We gave the third apple to Marc and, in between hungry bites, bombarded him with questions.

He told us as much as he knew about what had happened after we'd been thrown in with the chickens. 'I think Sister Bernadette was frightened at first – you know, frightened that Davie was dead. That man in charge of the gardens came in and got Davie out. He's a centenaire.' This was the Jersey equivalent of a community policeman. 'Told them to open the cupboard and he took him out. It was him had a good look at him and said he had just been knocked out, with the fall and all. Mind you, if Davie had been dead, I don't think he would have told anyone. They all stick together, that lot. Anyhow, he was still breathing so the man carried him up to the sick bay. And Sister Claire, who is really nice, is the one looking after him. He's going to be all right, Robbie.' He gasped for breath, his face red with the effort of providing so much information, and took a big bite out of his apple.

All I could take in was that he was alive and the relief I felt was so intense that I forgot for a few moments where we were and was almost happy.

Sister Claire came back all too soon to take Marc away and lock us in again but this time we weren't so scared. Our stomachs were full, my panic about Davie was over and we also felt that we had an ally; that not all of the adult world was against us.

We munched the rest of our food, washed it down with some of the milk and fell into another light doze.

Later on some more food was brought by one of the senior boys. This time it was our usual fare: jam sandwiches made from the hard brown bread that we were told was good for us.

Once the daylight faded and we were left completely in the dark our courage started to drain away. Every creak and rustle scared us, thoughts of the rats returned and we clutched each other in terror.

'Those nuns will have to calm down before they let us out,' Nicolas said miserably. 'They must be really angry.'

I wondered if what we had done really deserved a punishment as severe as this.

We huddled together with our backs against the wall and, despite our fear, exhaustion finally made us sleep.

It wasn't until the following morning that we were finally released. We heard the door being opened and hoped that it was Sister Claire, but it was Sister Freda who had come for us.

'Well, boys, have you had time to repent your sins and ask the good Lord for His forgiveness?' she asked. We noticed her smug satisfaction at seeing our tear-stained faces.

We swallowed any remaining pride, for we knew she was not someone we could fight against and win.

'Yes, Sister,' we said in unison. By that time we would have admitted to being guilty of any sin, as long it got us out of the barn.

She escorted us back to the main building, where she told us to go to the washrooms for a strip wash and get ready for mass. The task of cleaning the hall had been handed over to another group of boys. We were to be separated. In future Nicolas would work in the kitchen and I would have more work to do in the laundry.

'How is Davie? Is he all right, Sister?' I asked.

'He's in bed. He has a slight temperature. Apart from that he's fine,' she said, and I gave a huge sigh of relief. She told me that as soon as I had washed, put on clean clothes, been to mass and eaten breakfast, I could visit him for a few minutes before starting my new chores in the laundry.

He was fast asleep when I went into the sick room. I sat beside him, not certain what I should do. I thought of gently shaking him awake but was scared that I might hurt him.

As though sensing my presence, he stirred. His eyes opened and met mine. I smiled a huge smile for I was just so pleased to see him.

'Hi, Davie, are you all right?'

A faintly puzzled look crossed his face, his eyes shut and I knew he had fallen back to sleep again.

He stayed in the sick bay for a week. I went to see him every free moment. I sat at his bedside, talked to him and drew him pictures, but all I got in return was a vague, disinterested stare. He didn't laugh, he didn't cry, he just looked at me in the same slightly puzzled way before turning and falling back to sleep.

After a week he was sent back to the dormitory to be with us. I was still only six years old and too young to understand what had happened to him. All I knew about illness was what a pain in the stomach and a cold were. I'd certainly never heard of brain damage. It wasn't until I was an adult and the years of being in care were behind me that I was able to grasp what was wrong with Davie. His punishment for those few moments of fun in the hall was greater than any of us could comprehend back then.

That night I tossed and turned in my sleep gripped by a nightmare. I was in a huge room, devoid of furniture but full of dark shadows. Leaning against my legs was the warm body of my little brother. His fingers were tucked into my hand, his face turned up trustingly towards me.

The shadows shifted and from a dark corner a nun appeared. Her feet made no noise as she moved swiftly across the room. She came so close that I had to lean my head back to look up at her for she towered over us. My little brother's grip on my hand tightened, his eyes widened and I felt him tremble. I wanted to move, wanted us to get away from her, but as much as I tried, my feet refused to obey my silent command – run!

Her gaze held mine, compelling me to stay. As I stood there her eyes grew smaller and brighter. Her nose length-ened, grew sharper until it turned into a beak. She lifted up what I had thought were her arms but instead I saw to my horror they were huge wings; wings that spread out, wrapped themselves around Davie and started drawing him away from me.

I felt his fingers begin to slide out of my hand; he screamed; I tried vainly to hold onto him, and then he was gone from my grasp. More black human-sized crows appeared, their eyes glittering with a brilliant cruelty. The beat of their wings grew louder and louder and mixed with the muffled cries of my brother.

I tried to push through them but those wings formed an impenetrable barrier, then the crows lowered their heads and started pecking at my hands and arms, pecking and pecking. Davie's cries faded away until the pecking was the only sound left vibrating in my head. I opened my mouth to call out.

I woke.

Chapter Nineteen

Rain-filled dark clouds were replaced by flocks of small birds returning from faraway countries and the sun rose earlier, throwing golden rays through our dormitory windows. In the grounds the yellow heads of daffodils nodded gently, stirred by light, warm breezes. The boys working in the garden picked huge armfuls of them, divided these into smaller bunches and wrapped them in pretty paper. Groups of boys were given the job of piling them into a wheelbarrow and taking them into town to sell. The proceeds were for the orphanage. We all wanted this job because we were often given extra coins for ourselves by members of the public.

Easter weekend came and we had two weeks off school, but it also meant back-breaking work in the orphanage, hours of solemn Easter masses where we struggled to stay awake, and vigorous baths administered by the nuns. On the plus side there was a freshly boiled egg on Easter Sunday morning and, if we were lucky, a small piece of chocolate from the Easter eggs donated by kind people who thought the orphans deserved a treat.

The nuns had failed to indoctrinate me with their ardent religious beliefs. We were told repeatedly that the Sisters did God's work and obeyed his commands: commands that as far as I could see gave them the excuse to torment us and make our already miserable lives sheer hell. I asked myself why their God instructed them to be so cruel to us. That leather strap they all carried was used repeatedly on us. It caught me on the legs when they didn't think I had done my work well enough; on the back when my eyes had drooped during mass; or, as once happened, when I couldn't stop myself laughing out loud during the service. What had we done to make Him so angry?

If the nuns wanted us to know more about the religion that they told us was now ours, why were most of the sermons and all the masses in a language we could not understand?

The crucifixes and holy pictures that were liberally displayed in the orphanage showed such colossal anguish that they gave me gruesome nightmares. Behind my closed lids I saw that man coming down from the wooden cross, his damaged hands spattering blood and his mouth opened as he cried out in agony. I whimpered in sympathy, moisture leaked from my eyes and I awoke to find my pillow damp with tears.

After Davie's accident the nuns wouldn't let me work with Nicolas any more and they also decided I should be separated from Marc, because they knew he was a friend of mine. Marc and Nicolas were sent to work in the kitchen together and a new boy, Brian, was put in the laundry with me. Davie and Jimmy were given lighter tasks to do, usually under the concerned eyes of Sister Claire.

I liked having Brian working with me. He was a stocky, fair-haired boy with a round face and guileless blue eyes. When I asked why he was in there he told me that his mother was very ill and could no longer look after him. His father had left when Brian was still just a toddler. He couldn't remember him. There were no other relatives that his mother could have sent him to as she was an only child and both sets of grandparents had perished during the Blitz in London. He had to fend for himself and help with some household tasks such as shopping and carrying in the coal when she first became ill, but he could not stay on his own once she was hospitalised. The nuns had taken him to visit her at first, and prayers were said for her at mass, but one day she no longer recognised him when he sat at her bedside. He had cried all the way home from the hospital, and the nuns never took him again.

His lips quivered when he said that he hoped she would get better quickly so that he could go home again. The doctor had told him that she might not and that he must be brave. Somehow Brian didn't seem to understand what that could mean.

'She told me she loved me and that I must be good,' he said. 'And she gave me this.' From under his shirt he drew out a small gold locket. He flicked it open to reveal a tiny picture of a pretty blonde woman. The nuns had said he could wear the locket until he went to big school.

'She said I must keep it with me always till I get married. Then I can give it to my wife,' he said with an infectious giggle. I chortled back; at that age being a grown-up, let alone married, seemed a lifetime away.

Brian and I had quickly established a routine to make our work easier. We agreed to share the chores instead of each doing our own, and with the two of us scrubbing, rinsing and wringing together, the day seemed if not exactly to flash by, to pass more pleasantly. Between us we sorted the clothes into their various piles. We took turns doing the heavy, back-breaking job of rubbing the stained washing that the boiling had failed to clean. Up and down we scrubbed on those ridged boards until our hands were red and sore, but it was all made bearable by the odd moments when our eyes met and we burst into peals of chuckling. He became a good friend that summer when we were both trapped indoors doing one of the most unpopular jobs in the orphanage.

Working in the laundry, especially during the summer heat, was one of the most unpopular tasks and selling flowers was the most popular. But the only work that all of us were involved in was preparing for the summer fête. Every August, Sacre Coeur opened its gates to the public and held a fête that the nuns called 'Summerland'. It was the orphanage's biggest fund-raiser of the year and we children were its biggest asset. Preparations started in May but for the final two weeks it was all hands on deck to help with the final stages.

Groups of us, depending on our ages, were given different objects to make for the popular children's handicraft stall. Some of the older boys had learnt to stitch a variety of patterns over lines drawn on pieces of woollen material that were then turned into cushion covers. Others had been taught to knit squares of different colours that stitched together became colourful blankets, and the youngest – Brian, Davie, Jimmy, a couple of other little boys and I – were shown how to do French knitting.

We were given wooden cotton reels with four small gold-headed nails fixed to the top. Wool was then wound round them and, with a darning needle, we would pull it repeatedly over the nails making stitches as we went. Eventually a long knitted rope appeared at the bottom of the reel. As we became more agile with the needle it didn't take long before we were making yards of 'knitting'.

These ropes were then sent through to the girls' section where some were sewn into tablemats and others into slippers. We soon had a competition going amongst us to see who could make the longest rope in the shortest time. Davie was the slowest, his bottom lip protruding as he concentrated, while Jimmy surprised us by being the fastest.

There was an atmosphere of excitement throughout those weeks when we were preparing for the fête. Every child was in some way contributing towards its success and even the nuns seemed to be caught up with it and were less strict. They didn't try to stop us chattering quietly while we were making our various crafts.

The one job that every boy wanted was selling tickets to the public during the couple of weeks before the fête. Even though the nuns supervised the boys when they took them into town, they couldn't see everything that they did, especially when they were knocking on doors in residential streets and selling tickets door to door.

Because he was older, Nicolas was allowed to take a small group of boys to sell tickets in St Helier, under Sister Freda's supervision. The rest of us spent the day wondering how he had got on, envious of his freedom. When he came back his pockets were bulging with sweets that he shared with Marc, Davie, Brian and me.

'Where did you get them?' I asked.

'People give them to us. They gave me extra money as well. I'm going to see if you can come with me the next time I go,' he said. 'It's great. I'll tell the nice French Sister that people like to buy their tickets from the littlest ones.'

Whatever he said to convince them I don't know, but I was allowed out with Nicolas and Marc the next time they went.

'The secret,' Nicolas told me, 'is to look for holiday-makers, especially those who look near the end of it. You'll know who they are because they have a suntan! Otherwise, try and spot the day-trippers; they're even better. Most times they won't want a ticket 'cos they won't still be here for the fête. But they give you money for the orphanage – maybe as much as a shilling! The trick is that you have to look as though you've put it in the collection box.' He showed me how to tuck a coin in the palm of my hand, hold it in place with my thumb and jerk the box so that the coins gave a satisfactory little clink.

'That's our money for sweets and stuff,' he said.

'Now here's our patter: the tickets are a florin each, the money goes to help run the orphanage, there's handicrafts that all of the children have made, there's a choir, and there's loads of stalls where you can win things or buy things and of course we've all helped, because it's our home.'

He laughed at the disbelieving look on my face. 'It works! Those day-trippers and holidaymakers almost feel guilty that they won't be here to see the poor little orphans sing and dance for them. They nearly always give us something. If you get good at it we can buy ice-cream and take sweets back for Davie too.'

'How do we get away from the nuns?' Marc asked.

'We walk beside a tourist for a bit until we can get round a corner. They talk to us and the nun thinks that's because they are buying lots of tickets,' laughed Nicolas.

It was Marc who pushed me in the direction of the first middle-aged couple, and shyly I went up to them. I clutched the tickets in my outstretched hand. I had forgotten my sales pitch and all I managed to say that anyone could have understood was 'fête' and 'orphan'. I knew my face was bright red and even my ears felt fiery with embarrassment.

The woman bent down to my height and gave me a warm smile. She looked up at her smiling husband, whose nose was pink and peeling from the warm Jersey sun, with a questioning look. 'Well, young man,' he said, 'we will have two tickets.' He gave me four shillings that I dropped through the slot in my collecting tin and I tore off two tickets for them. 'And here's one and sixpence for you and your friends,' he added, pressing the coins into the palm of my outstretched hand.

Marc and Nicolas beamed at me when, still flushed, I ran up to them clutching my booty.

'Blimey, didn't take you long to get the hang of it. Go and sell some more, got to keep those nuns happy, then we'll go and have ice-cream,' said Nicolas. I puffed up with pride.

Bold with my initial success, I went up to every couple I could find. My blushes stopped and I managed to get all the words out and smile back at them confidently. Every person I approached bought tickets. Another two people gave me sixpence for ice-cream. Several patted me on top of my head. I felt good.

St Helier's streets and lanes were familiar territory: the colourful hanging baskets outside the shops, the cobbles underfoot, the warm sunshine and the shops selling all the things tourists loved to buy. For a day it was as if we were not part of Sacre Coeur, but just boys out in the town, laughing and ragging each other. I felt some of the same exhilarating sense of freedom that I had known the previous summer. But then I felt an almost physical pain because as those memories flooded back I suddenly realised just how much I still missed John. I knew Stanley was in hospital but I wondered if I might see Gloria anywhere. Why hadn't she come back for us all? But I never saw so much as a glimpse of her.

The day of the fête arrived and the gates were opened to the public. All of us were going to help with the stalls, mostly behind the scenes replenishing stock and carrying trays of food out.

'Robbie,' said Sister Bernadette to me at breakfast, 'I've heard you're quite the salesman.' My mouth hung open at something that sounded like praise coming from her. 'You can work on the handicraft stall.' My face must have lit up for that was one of the better jobs.

'And Robbie?' she paused.

'Yes, Sister.'

'Take Brian with you. His mother died this morning.'

I sold a lot of handicrafts that day and Brian helped me. Sister Bernadette had told him that his mother was now in heaven. I don't think he knew where heaven was.

Chapter Twenty

Shortly after that the summer holidays ended and it was time for me to move up into the Juniors. Davie and Jimmy were to start in the Infants.

As we walked to school, I suddenly saw how much my little brother had changed. Where once he had been round, now he was thin. His shoulder blades pressed against the fabric of his coarse shirt. His neck, once ringed with little rolls of puppy fat, was now so slender it hardly looked strong enough to hold up his head. Even his legs had lost their roundness and looked almost stick-like, with blue veins showing through almost translucent skin.

As well as looking different on the outside there were differences on the inside. Whereas before the accident he was often demanding and unhappy, now it seemed that the Davie I knew, both the irritating and the lovable sides, had completely gone.

There was a lack of connection. If I tickled him he didn't squirm or chortle with laughter. Instead he would just lie limply, his eyes looking at me with complete indifference. He never laughed, and the constant tears that had once annoyed me so much seemed to have dried up completely. A blank passiveness had replaced the emotions of grief, rage and occasional amusement that used to chase across his little face. He still had a deep connection with his friend Jimmy but I hardly ever heard them talking to each other.

When we arrived at school that first day back, Sister Claire took the little boys in the direction of the Infants and pushed me gently towards the more imposing doors that led to the Juniors.

'You go in there now, Robbie,' she instructed, 'and I'll see you at four o'clock.'

My new teacher, Mr Douglas, looked impatient at my lateness when I entered his classroom. I recognised my fellow classmates from the last term in the Infants, but they ignored me as usual. I saw Mr Douglas's gaze sweep over me and I felt a sinking sensation. I recognised that look. It spoke more loudly to me than if he had said it out loud: 'Bastard! I don't like bastards in my class.'

I knew that the relative safety of the Infants had come to an end. This tall, thin man with sparse, greying hair and a thin little mouth obviously had no sympathy for the boys from Sacre Coeur.

My eyesight was very poor. In the Infants I had always managed to sit near the front of the class, but here all the other children had arrived early to claim their desk places so I was seated at the back. The blackboard and the writing on it was just a blur and classes that I had once enjoyed when sitting at the front now almost reduced me to tears.

'You, Garner!' Mr Douglas would demand at the beginning of the arithmetic class. 'What's the answer to that sum?'

However much I squinted at the board, the figures were indistinguishable. The first time it happened I tried to tell him that I couldn't see what was on the board.

'Oh, for goodness sake, boy,' was his response. 'If you don't know the answer, don't waste my time – just say so.' And for greater emphasis he slapped a ruler into the unturned palm of his hand.

'I don't know, sir,' I would reply unhappily, my eyes cast down. He walked up the aisle, still smacking his ruler repeatedly into his hand, until he stood next to me. I could feel the warmth of him right next to my elbow.

'Don't know much, do you, Garner? Well, you had better start learning. There will be no dunces in my class.'

I wanted to tell him that the reason I couldn't give him the answers was that I couldn't see the board, but after one look at his scowling face I held my tongue. Taking my silence as further proof of my uselessness (although if I had spoken up he would have labelled me as impertinent), he flicked the ruler viciously across my knuckles and walked away.

We orphans were still fed separately and were very seldom allowed into the playground to mix with the other children. On the nuns' insistence we were sent to do our homework during the breaks. I am sure this was just another way of making sure that we remained separated from the temptations of the outside world.

The other children jeered at us when we passed them in the corridor. I heard words like 'bastard' many times, and by quizzing the older boys at the home I quickly learnt what it meant. I noticed that the teachers who overheard these jeers seldom stopped or reprimanded the boys responsible.

Boys can be cruel. They love tormenting those who are different, and we were undoubtedly different. Itching powder was brought into school hidden in the pockets of satchels and stealthily removed during class. It was sprinkled down the back of a victim's shirt or, even worse, trousers, then the perpetrator and his cronies would chortle with glee. The first time it happened to me I let out a small shriek as I felt the stinging itch. It was as though I had stepped into a clump of nettles, and I jumped up trying to scratch the inflamed part of my body. The class was in an uproar. Boys doubled over laughing and Mr Douglas turned from the board and marched down the aisle.

'It's you, isn't it, Garner? Not content with being stupid you want to play the fool and disrupt my class completely. I suppose you were never taught manners, not where you must have come from.' His hand shot out, caught my ear and forcibly pulled me from my seat. My ear hurt, my back was stinging unbearably and I could hear the sniggers of my classmates as he marched me to the front.

'Bend over,' he barked.

His hand pushed me hard until my chest was flat on his desk and my toes were just scraping the floor. He held me there for a few seconds swishing his cane in the air and allowing my fear to build. I heard his clothes rustle as he raised it, the whoosh it made as he brought it down and then felt searing pain. 'Six of the best, Garner,' he said with satisfaction, as he brought the cane down again and again.

The class had gone quiet. Everyone there knew that, although he liked the orphans least, none of them was immune from his rage. That first time he caned me I wept as I walked back to my desk. This hurt more than when Sister Freda had whipped me with her strap and it was made even worse by being humiliated in front of my peers.

Being the only boy in the class from the orphanage seemed to make me Mr Douglas's favourite target. He knew there was no one to listen to my complaints. The nuns didn't care and I had no parents to stick up for me.

I had to work out my own ways of getting by. Homework questions were always written on the board for us to copy down. I would wait till the other children had left before I came forward to write down the details. My homework was almost always correct because I was terrified of being punished again. Mr Douglas would return my dog-eared exercise book grudgingly, saying, 'Did you get help, Garner?' 'No, sir,' I'd whisper in reply, wondering where he thought I could possibly get help from.

I tried to be as inconspicuous as possible. I worked hard and memorised my times tables and I learnt simple addition so that I could get my sums right, but this only seemed to infuriate him more.

'Garner, are you paying attention?' he would call out when I was peering short-sightedly at the board. 'Yes, sir,' I would answer, praying that reply would satisfy him.

'What's the answer to that sum, then?' I would fall silent. I could hear my classmates sniggering and my ears would start to burn.

I remain convinced that he knew I had bad eyesight and knew that unless he called the figures out I couldn't possibly know the answers.

'Cat got that tongue of yours, has it?' he would say in false tones of disgust and, if in a good mood, he would content himself with giving me a whack round the head. If in a bad one, it would be a vice-like grip on my ear, a wrench, followed by the hiss of the cane as it descended. All the time I could hear him chanting, 'Lazy, stupid boy. What are you, Garner? Tell me, what are you?'

'I'm a lazy, stupid boy,' I would repeat.

At that age that's what I believed I was.

Chapter Twenty-one

For some time I had not had to work with Neville because of the long hours I worked in the laundry with Brian. Eventually Sister Freda noticed our friendship, and she disapproved.

'Seeing you two seem to get on so well together you can both go and work with Neville on Saturday,' she announced.

She had a hatred of seeing any Sacre Coeur boys enjoying themselves. When the visitors came and we had to present a happy front I would often catch her looking at us with her mouth tucked firmly in and a look of bitter discontent on her face. She would stand close to a boy and put her arm across his shoulder, in an apparently affectionate gesture, then her fingers would swiftly nip the soft underside of his upper arm. Whatever love she was capable of feeling for her religion it certainly didn't extend to the little boys who were in her care.

I sighed. I knew that Sister Freda was fully aware of how much I hated it there, even though I did my best to hide my horror of that room from her.

'Both of you come to me as soon as you have finished your breakfast, and don't dawdle on the way.'

'Yes, Sister,' was all I said meekly.

Brian and I followed as she marched purposefully down corridors and across the playground to the chicken-killing rooms. There was no time for me to warn Brian what awaited him.

'We've got you a new boy today, Neville,' she said, standing in the doorway.

I realised for the first time that she never crossed the threshold. Maybe even she got squeamish when faced with the reality of how the chickens that ended up on her dinner plate were killed.

'I know you need the help,' she said as she pushed us firmly through the door. I heard the rustling of her habit as she moved away and then the sound of Neville's breathing.

'Robbie,' he said, a note of excitement in his voice, 'I've got something to show you.' I shuddered and tried to avoid looking at him. He stretched his fat arm out and patted my wrist. 'Come, you're going to like it. Bring your friend as well.'

What had he got planned for this week? What new method of torment had he conjured up for us? But this time he surprised me. He opened a door that had always been locked when I'd been there before.

'Go on, go in,' he said.

The sight that met my eyes when I looked in instantly dispersed my fear. A score or more of spindly-legged, tiny yellow chicks were running round the brightly lit room.

'They've only just hatched,' Neville said with a note of pride in his voice. 'Look!' In the middle of the room I saw what looked like a large tray with a glass top fixed to it. The inside was packed with chicken eggs.

'It's an incubator. That's where the eggs go until the baby chickens are ready to come out. They started hatching this morning.'

Open-mouthed, Brian and I watched as black cracks gradually appeared on egg after egg. I heard Brian give a little gasp as the shells fell apart, releasing creamy yellow chicks. To us it seemed that they entered the world cheeping with the same excitement we felt watching them. Some were already dipping minute beaks into the food that was waiting for them.

'There will be a hundred of them soon,' Neville told us, still with that note of pride in his voice. 'They're nice and warm in here. When they've grown a little bit I'll take them to another home. Got to keep them separate from the bigger birds for a while.'

He scooped one up in his huge hands and gently stroked the downy feathers. 'They're like us, Robbie – no mum or dad to look after them.' Then, with an abrupt change of mood and subject, he said, 'Your Davie – he's just like me now.'

What did he mean? Davie wasn't horrible and cruel like him. I knew what he was implying, though; the change in Davie was obvious. He still had the puzzled look he'd had the week after the accident. He was slow to respond to questions and I never heard him laugh any more. But whatever Davie had become, he was not like Neville and never would be, I told myself fiercely.

'Yes, he's like me now. But he's not ugly like me. Not pretty little Davie,' Neville continued as though he had read my mind. An expression flashed across his face, an expression I had never seen before: maybe a sad awareness of who he really was. I met his eyes and saw it just for that fleeting moment and then it was gone, leaving the mixture of spite and glee I was used to.

Maybe if I had been older I might have seen the boy he still was, condemned to a life imprisoned in a fat man's body; might have recognised the isolation that his ugliness and lack of intelligence had enforced upon him. Maybe I would have accepted his temper tantrums more readily, as one tolerates a two-year-old's frustrated outburst when thwarted. Maybe I would have seen his sexual groping as being a sad attempt to satisfy a desire that he was incapable of expressing or fulfilling in an adult way. But at seven years of age, all I saw was a fat, ugly man with an adult's power over us, who both frightened and repelled me.

We left that room with the chirping, pretty little chicks and Neville led us back into the chicken-killing rooms. Everything in there was the same as it was most Saturdays. Bunches of squirming chickens hung from hooks, the tin bath was on the floor and the bowl for collecting blood to sprinkle on the gardens was standing ready.

'Basin needs filling,' Neville said curtly, pointing to the tin bath.

Brian kept sneaking questioning glances at me, his eyes wide with surprise, as he helped me to fill the large basin with boiling water from the geyser.

Neville smiled at Brian, a smile I recognised all too well. He was pleased to have a new audience who he could disgust and frighten.

'Watch this, Brian,' he said, and out came the knife; off came the first head, blood spurted, the wings flapped frantically even in death, and Brian visibly blanched.

Neville giggled with excitement and cut one bunch of chickens down. The birds raced round the room in the mistaken belief that they were free. That was a game Neville loved. He laughed out loud before catching one bird and slitting its throat. There was a look of such gloating pleasure on his face as he watched the headless bird flap its wings and totter for a few steps before it fell that I felt sick. I saw the horror on Brian's face suddenly change and be replaced by one of fury.

'Stop that!' he yelled, and ran over to Neville. His arms swung back and, because he couldn't reach any higher, he punched Neville in the stomach. 'You bleeding loony,' he shrieked. 'You bleeding wicked bastard! I'll tell the nuns on you.'

For a few moments Neville's face wore a shocked expression, one that changed swiftly to outrage. For all his size he moved fast. He stepped sideways to avoid the next punch, caught Brian's arm as it swung and, with a quick twist, wrenched it high behind the boy's back. His fat knee came up and connected with Brian's bottom, propelling him forward. Neville picked him up, shook him so hard that Brian's head was bobbing from side to side, then, using Brian's jumper as a loop, he hung him on a hook.

'Now you can hang with the chickens,' Neville said, and giggled.

I wanted to help but knew that anything I did would only make the situation worse.

Brian's face was scarlet with rage, and he was flailing with his arms and legs in an attempt to reach some part of Neville. When he realised Neville was too far back he twisted in the air, then wriggled and bucked, trying to release himself. Finally the struggling stopped when he realised he was completely trapped.

The expression on Neville's face changed to one I recognised and I knew that Brian's utter helplessness had aroused him. His meaty hand snaked up the leg of Brian's trousers. I could see the outline of his hands as they inched round and knew that he had my friend's tiny penis in his hand. Neville's other arm wrapped itself around the boy's small body, drawing him closer and, without being able to see, I knew that his fat pudgy fingers had slipped up the back of Brian's trousers to stroke and knead his small buttocks. I felt shame that I hadn't managed to warn Brian about this, but I don't think I could have put it into words. It was all too disgusting.

Unlike me, Brian fought back. His face contorted with anger, he shouted, struggled and swore. Neville giggled and moved his fleshy hands faster. I think it was the giggle that did it for Brian. He made a coughing sound at the back of his throat, sucked in his cheeks then spat a gob of spit and phlegm as hard as he could into Neville's fat face.

'You bleeding ugly queer,' he screamed. 'Get your bloody hands off me, you fat stupid bastard.' His foot kicked out hard and caught Neville in the chest. 'My mum warned me about men like you.'

That was when Neville completely lost control. Bellow after bellow of such primal fury left his saliva-flecked mouth that I shrank against the wall. Nearly indistinguishable words were mixed in with his shouts and I could only vaguely hear snatches of what he said. 'Bastard, bastard', 'A lesson you'll not forget' and again 'bastard'. He was utterly consumed with rage; his huge, sweating body seemed to become even more swollen.

The colour drained from Brian's face as he watched Neville look round the room for some instrument he could use to inflict pain. I saw where his gaze landed and with a terrible shock I suddenly knew what he was going to do. I wanted to do something, anything to stop him, but I was rooted to the spot with my own fear.

Neville spun round with a demonic look on his face and I watched as he knelt down and picked up the bath of still steaming, almost boiling water.

Every last vestige of colour drained from Brian's face, his head jerked from side to side and his eyes bulged with terror. His mouth opened and whimpering pleas left it. 'Please, please,' he begged. 'Don't.'

Neville laughed at him, a high-pitched shrill giggle that made the hairs on the back of my neck stand up.

'No!' I shouted, with a voice that roared within but came out puny and high-pitched from terror.

The water left the bath in a silvery arc. It drenched Brian's stomach and shoulders. There was a dreadful scream that seemed to go on and on and was followed by an appalling silence. I closed my eyes but not before I had seen clouds of steam rising from Brian's body; a body that was hanging limply from the hook, with water running off it and forming a pool under his twitching, dangling legs.

The silence that followed frightened me even more than the screaming had; I found I was huddled on the floor, my knees drawn into my body and my hands protecting my ears. I don't know how long I was there before the door burst open. Suddenly there were grown-up voices, hands touched me and they took me to another room where I sat, very still, very scared.

After a while Sister Bernadette came. She told me that Neville had been taken away. She said that Brian was being looked after. She gave me a slice of cake to eat and a glass of milk to drink. She said I must forget what I had seen. Her being nice scared me more than anything else.

I waited anxiously for Brian to reappear, worried about the burns he must have suffered. I kept trying to ask the nuns where he was, but even Sister Claire didn't give me an answer. After a while I stopped asking but although I never spoke of it again I didn't stop wondering.

Chapter Twenty-two

Over the next three years nothing very much changed in my life, either at Sacre Coeur or at school. Every day was fraught with the underlying threat of violence, both verbal and physical. I went to school and was bullied. I did my chores in the mornings and evenings plus all day at weekends and during the school holidays, all under the gaze of the nuns. Sometimes it was the hot, steamy laundry room, other times the chilly gardens where we had the back-breaking job of breaking up the clumps of water-sodden soil in preparation for the sowing of seeds. Six of us had to pull a huge sheet of metal with sharp barbs on the underside to rake the earth and create narrow funnels. I'd seen carthorses do this before, but never human beings. It seemed to us that the nuns took a perverse delight in making us work in the laundry on hot days and the gardens on the cold ones.

Three years of being the butt of jokes, three years of being caned and mocked by Mr Douglas, three years of long hours of back-breaking chores and three years of crying into my pillow. Three years before a series of events made me change forever.

The first significant event was when it was recognised that I needed glasses. Seeing me peering at my exercise book, a relief teacher took it upon himself to take me for an eye test. The disadvantage of being called 'four eyes' was by far outweighed by my sudden ability to see the blackboard and everything around me with clarity for the first time.

Mine was now the first hand that shot up in class. 'Oh, not you again, Garner,' Mr Douglas would complain. He still thought of new ways to torment me, but getting the answers right at least gave me a degree of protection from his sarcastic tongue.

The second event was when I was chosen to be part of the new gymnastics team. For the first time the orphanage had an organiser, a man named Dennis. Just under six foot tall, he had thick, dark, wavy hair, swept straight back from a low forehead. His bright blue eyes under heavy black brows twinkled when he caught us looking at him and an ever-ready smile made him a person we felt we could talk to. Apart from the priests and our schoolteachers, we had few adult male role models. Dennis was just the sort of man that young boys felt they could look up to. Thick cords of muscle ran up his arms, his shoulders were broad, his legs were thick and his long strides jaunty. He was the sort of man we aspired to grow up to be.

Dennis told us that he was a plumber in the daytime but that he was free in the evenings and at weekends. Sport was his passion, he told us repeatedly, and it was sport that turned boys into men. He would train us to put on a gymnastics show for the next summer fête.

He said he needed twenty boys in all. The team would consist of six of the older ones, eight aged between eight and ten, and six of the youngest boys.

'All for the glory of God,' the nuns said. They felt they were lucky having someone like Dennis who had volunteered his services. 'He has been sent to us by the blessed Mary,' they told us knowingly.

I saw him talking to them, looking earnestly down at their upturned faces as they gazed back at him. On those occasions even Sister Freda's face broke out into a big smile and I saw Sister Claire's hand cover her mouth as she tried to stop a girlish giggle escaping. Dennis, it seemed, had every nun under his spell.

Apart from Jimmy and Davie there was not a boy in the orphanage who didn't want to be in the gymnastics team. We were tired of doing what we thought of as girls' things in preparation for the fête – all the knitting and crafts and helping the nuns to prepare mountains of food to be sold and consumed on the day.

Also, however busy we were with whichever task we had been allocated, we were always aware of the nuns' sharp eyes watching us. They always found time to inspect our work, looking for any fault they could find. Should they find anything that they felt was not up to their exacting standards then a cuff around the head or stinging flick of the strap would come our way.

But if we were chosen for the team, not only would we be excused many of the weekend and evening chores as the fête drew close, but in the new colourful sports outfit we would be given, we felt we would be 'someone'. That someone would be part of a show, that someone would receive applause, that someone would be noticed and admired.

Dennis stopped me in the corridor. 'Robbie,' he said, 'hello there!' While I had noticed him, I was surprised he had noticed me and actually knew my name.

'I've watched you,' he said, 'with your digging and working in the gardens. You move well, boy. How would you like to be in the gymnastics team?'

Would I! 'Yes,' I said, 'I would. But,' and my hand nervously indicated my glasses.

'This here's not football, boy,' was his response. 'Come, let me show you something.'

He took my arm, held it in a strong grip and led me down a corridor to a room I had never seen before. He opened the door and, with his hand on my shoulder, guided me in.

'Here it is!' he said, his voice almost vibrating with pride, and something else that made me flinch slightly. His hand moved up to my neck, gripped it lightly and his fingers stroked the soft down at the back of my neck. I tried to shrug them away and suddenly I wanted to leave, but didn't know how to without seeming rude.

'Now, boy,' he said, 'I want you to take your glasses off.' I did as he said and put them carefully in my pocket.

'What can you see?'

I told him the truth: I could see everything but it was all just a bit fuzzy. Letters were the main problem; a moving ball was also very difficult, but something that did not move and was large was easy.

'You can see the vaulting horse, can't you? Yes? Well, if you can see it, you can jump over it.' I had a try and Dennis seemed pleased. 'You're light and you're fast,' I was told.

It was so important to me to be in that team that I was prepared to overcome my instinctive uneasiness. It was just so flattering for me to be singled out for something and told that I was good at it. Praise wasn't something I was used to.

When the team had been selected, we met for the first practice session. We were to be trained to do a full gymnastics show. We started with a simple bar display, where we swung and moved in unison. After that it was the vaulting horse. For that, dressed just in shorts and a vest, we were lined up in a neat formation in order of height, took a short run to gain speed, put our hands out and vaulted right over the horse. The finale of the show was a human pyramid. The bigger boys were on the bottom and the youngest and smallest one was at the very top.

We started our training as planned in May. It was only once a week to begin with, but as the summer came we had to practise much more often.

Two older teenage boys, who were long-term inmates of Sacre Coeur, were Dennis's assistants.

Was it complete naivety on the part of the nuns that they didn't see the darker side of Dennis? Did the desire to make the fête different and more spectacular blind them to his faults and foibles? I don't know, but we boys soon found out what they were.

For a treat, some of the boys were allowed to watch television in Dennis room. The nuns trusted him to make the right choice of programme for us. The first time I went there, he gave me sweets. The second time, his trousers came off. He told us to do the same, and there was something so powerful about Dennis that he didn't have to lift a threatening hand to make us do as he wanted.

His large hand would first pat our knees, stroke a head, and then ask if we wanted more sweets. Yes, we did. Small hands would be grasped and fingers wrapped around a penis that to my child's eyes looked red and angry. Cigarettes and soft drinks appeared. The first time I lit a cigarette I coughed, but I grew to like the sensation of inhaling smoke. I liked the feeling of being part of a group.

I didn't like touching Dennis's penis. 'It's nice, Robbie,' he said, as his fingers touched mine. I sucked my sweet and wanted to leave.

Could I have told the nuns what he was doing? Could any of us? Or would they think we were lying or even beat us for being a 'Devil's child'? We thought that if we told, those leather straps would rain down on us, dark cupboard doors would open and the stench of the deep litter barns would fill our nostrils all over again. And we were far too ashamed to discuss it amongst ourselves.

He abused all of us in turn. He made us suck him, fondle and rub; we listened to his groans, watched his face grow red and his eyes shut as he leant back in the chair, revelling in his own pleasure.

Dennis had us in his power, and his two assistants were bullies who stood with splayed legs, hands on hips and a sneer on their lips as we practised our jumps and lifts in the makeshift gymnasium.

'Jump!' he would shout at a boy. 'Jump higher!'

Jimmy was the smallest boy who had been chosen, and for him it was a nightmare. He hadn't wanted to do gymnastics and didn't like being part of the group. At the vaulting practice he missed the box, his knees hit the side and he crumpled to the floor.

'I'm going to show you what happens to little boys who keep missing the horse,' Dennis told him. His two side-kicks snickered.

Jimmy looked at Dennis blankly. 'It's too high for me,' he said in his high-pitched, childish tones.

Dennis lifted the top part of the box off. He beckoned us forward so that we could see what he was doing. There were three tiers to that wooden vaulting horse and Dennis took the top one off and placed it on the floor.

'If you can't go over it you can go inside it for the rest of the training session,' he said to a cringing Jimmy. He scooped him up and placed him on a small shelf inside. He pushed him forward so that his bottom was high in the air and strapped his wrists to a rung at floor level so he was almost upside down. The top went back on and Dennis picked up a flagpole that was used on the playing field to mark out jumps. He poked it hard through the hand hole in the side of the box, laughing as he did so.

'That's the punishment for boys who won't jump,' he told all of us, then handed the pole to one of his assistants. 'You do it; not too hard, though – don't want to skewer him.'

Jimmy was the first one to receive that punishment, but over the weeks it was to be meted out to most of us. It was painful and humiliating. Each time it happened, however young we were, the last shreds of our self-worth were forcibly removed.

When Jimmy was let out he didn't cry or say anything. I remembered him the first time I'd seen him, that first night in the chapel when a nun pushed him off the bench. He was such a sad, lonely little boy who wanted his mother not to be dead, and his father to come back to Jersey for him.

His silence seemed to outrage Dennis and, just as Mr Douglas had picked me out to bully at school, so Dennis now picked on Jimmy. He told the nuns that he refused to jump. 'But,' he said, 'every boy in this group must do something.' The nuns nodded their heads in agreement.

'You are going to learn a song, Jimmy,' he told him. 'One that suits you. "Hang down your head, Tom Dooley" seems the right one, and you are going to sing it for the visitors at the fête. You, my boy, are going to do the solo.'

I wonder how Dennis knew that he had chosen the worst possible punishment for the quiet, timid and insular Jimmy.

Jimmy was no match for Dennis physically, but he knew he wouldn't be able to go through with it. As the fête approached, he left his bed in the middle of the night and dragged his sheet along the corridor to the gym. In the dark he climbed the bars, tied the sheet round his neck and secured the other end around the top bar. Unlike Stanley, he managed to tie the knot correctly.

He was found early the next morning, his small face suffused with blood, his tongue protruding from a mouth that had seldom smiled and faeces and urine streaking his legs.

I don't know where he was buried.

Davie never asked where his friend was. I think somehow he must have known.

Chapter Twenty-three

There is, I found, a limit to the amount of humiliation you are prepared to take. There is an end to fear. There is the start of anger.

My anger began as a tiny spark but it took three years before it turned into a flame. And when it did, I found that I was no longer afraid. What was the final straw that ignited it? I don't know, but Jimmy's death certainly changed something in me.

Dennis left after Jimmy died. He was seen coming out of Sister Bernadette's office, his face bright red with anger. His teenage cronies helped him pack up his car and he drove off without a word to anybody else. I wonder what organisation that worked with young children he wormed his way into next?

His bullying assistants started a rumble of excuses that they spewed out loudly for all to hear, trying to absolve themselves from any blame.

Nobody talked about the compartment in the vaulting horse. Nobody mentioned Jimmy's fear: the fear that had crept under the little boy's skin, bleaching it a ghostly white; the fear that had made his muscles twitch and quiver and his heart beat faster and faster; the fear that curled round his throat, restricting his breathing until he gasped for breath; the fear that he had ended with a rope. No, nobody talked about that.

'He missed his dead mother,' the bullies said. 'It's his father's fault for leaving him here.' And the final words of self-justification: 'He wasn't quite right in the head. Couldn't have been, could he?' Each time they repeated their remarks, their own belief in them grew and, once believed completely, they turned their attention to the next potential victim of their cruelty.

I watched them, those boys, as they swaggered along corridors; bullies, I noticed, always went about in groups. They picked on the insular boys, the ones with few friends to protect them. They craved the admiration of their peers and the palpable fear of the weak. Then another realisation came to me: bullies were also cowards.

'Four eyes,' a boy at school called me. 'You think you're a smarty-pants, first hand up with the answer every time,' said another. 'Bastard!' was the next insult that assaulted my ears. My shoulders hunched up in the familiar victim's cringe. I wanted to get past them before a foot came out to trip me, a finger poked me painfully in the ribs, or I was pinched spitefully on a soft spot of my body. I started to put my head down, started to scurry past – and then I stopped.

For the first time I turned and drew myself up to my full height.

'Sod that,' I said to myself and took my glasses off.

I looked at my main tormentor. Without my glasses, the boy was blurred but I could see enough to shoot my fist out. I suddenly remembered John protecting me once. 'Hit hard on the shoulder first,' he'd told me, and that was what I did. With a look of stunned incredulity, my tormentor stumbled back.

'What did you just call me?' I asked and the bully paused for a second, sensing something had changed in me.

'Bastard, a sorry little bastard,' he repeated and squared up to me.

I pulled my fist back twice more and slammed it into the bully's stomach, winding him. I heard his breath leave his body in an astonished whoosh, and then my fist connected with his chin. He went down. It all happened so fast that by the time a teacher realised something was happening, it was over. His companions had already slunk quietly away down the corridor.

'I slipped, sir,' the boy said and Mr Douglas chose to believe that story.

That was the start of my fighting back.

I went to the school gym and had a word with the sports master. 'I want to train for sports day,' I told him. 'I want to be part of it.'

He remembered me trying out for the football team and missing even the easiest of kicks, so he gave me a dubious look.

'My eyesight might not be good enough for football,' I said, looking unflinchingly up into his face. 'But,' I repeated Dennis's words, 'I'm fast and I'm light. Without my glasses I can't see the numbers on a blackboard or a moving ball, but I can run. I can run fast!'

He smiled. 'Can you, lad? All right, Garner, I'm going to give you a chance. You can start training with the relay team.'

A smile stretched my face from ear to ear.

'Oh, and Garner – no more fights; not if you want to stay in the team.'

'No, sir.'

It was just after I started training for the relay team that something amazing happened. I was out working in the gardens, and during our mid-morning break one of the boys had pulled me to one side.

'Robbie, make some excuse, say you've got an upset stomach, have to go to the lav, got the runs, anything. Your brother's just on the other side of the wall, behind the outhouses.'

'What? He can't be!' I was sure he must be mistaken. Davie would be inside dusting the hall at that time.

'Your big brother. What's his name? John,' the boy said.

My heart jumped. I felt a tingly sensation all over my body. Could it be? Could it really be?

I hurriedly did what had been suggested; I doubled over groaning loudly, clasping my stomach. I said I had the runs, and when the nun on duty grudgingly gave me permission to leave, I staggered to the lavatory door as convincingly as I could. Luckily the section of the wall behind the lavatories was lower than the rest and didn't have spikes embedded in it.

As soon as I knew I was out of sight of the main building, I ran as fast as my feet would carry me. When I rounded a corner I saw him sitting on top of the wall.

It was not the John I remembered, not the boy of eight whose picture I had so often reached for in my mind, but the John he had grown into, who was now thirteen; with his broad shoulders, muscular arms, and a face that had lost all trace of childish innocence, he already looked like a young man.

A huge smile spread across his tanned face and his pale grey eyes sparkled as he looked down at me.

'Robbie,' he said softly.

On seeing that smile that made his eyes crinkle up at the corners, that smile that had always said 'It's just you and me, brother,' I felt the prickle of tears and swallowed hard. Now was not the time to cry. I wanted him to jump down, to hug me – but big boys don't do that, I told myself sternly. I dashed the back of my hand across my face, flicked aside a tear and whooped in glee.

'Hello, John,' I said and swung myself up next to him.

'You've grown tall,' he remarked. 'You jumped up here without any help.' He looked me up and down admiringly.

He told me he had borrowed a bicycle from one of the wardens at Haut de la Garenne. I found out later that he might have borrowed it, but it certainly wasn't with permission.

It was the first time he had been able to get to the orphanage, he told me. He had wanted to all right, he had missed us terribly, but it had been difficult to get out of the home.

'It's not so bad now,' he said, 'now I'm a bit older. But they kept an eye on us when we were younger.'

He asked about Denise and Davie. I told him I'd never found out where Denise was but said that Davie was fine. I couldn't tell him about the accident; not yet anyway.

He told me his plans then. 'I've only got just over a year left in that place, then I can get a job and live in a hostel. There's a man there, he's not too bad, he's the one fixes everything up. Once I'm out of there they won't be able to stop me visiting you here. Then it won't be much longer till you get out and we can get a place together. I'll be old enough to get Davie out too, you see if I don't.'

His words swept over me like warm rays of sunshine. I imagined all three of us in a small sunny flat, with money coming in to put food on the table, nice clothes, and trips to the beach together again. The pictures he drew filled my head with wonderful images that day.

He told me he would try to come again. Nothing was easy, though. I had to keep my chin up and I had to send his love to Davie. All of a sudden he was gone, pedalling back to the home.

I went to bed that night with my secret curled up warmly inside of me. I knew it couldn't be shared. I knew I couldn't tell Davie even though I wanted to so badly because he wouldn't understand that it had to be kept secret. The day that only that morning had seemed so grey and drab, a day like any other, had just for a short while been changed immeasurably.

As I lay in bed I could still hear his voice, see the picture of the person he was now, and hear him promising me the one thing I wanted more than anything else – a future and a family. I had no doubt he could make this happen because he seemed so grown-up now. His voice had already broken and the tones were deep and resonant in comparison to my squeaky childlike voice. A soft down already topped his upper lip and he had thick blond hair on his arms and legs as well. I was so proud because he looked more like a man than a boy, and took great delight in telling the other boys that he was my brother.

I saw John twice more. He came to the wall and together we made our plans. Then he stopped coming and it was a whole year before I found out why, and it would be almost four years before I saw him again.

Chapter Twenty-four

As the school's sports day drew closer, everyone was excited and it was the main topic of conversation at break time. I felt huge waves of exhilaration because for the first time ever I was going to be part of a school event. I had been chosen to try out for the relay team. Permission had been sought from the nuns and surprisingly granted for me to practise once a week. I could hardly wait.

The children who had been at the school longer explained some of the events to me. Sports day was a family affair where parents often joined in with the infant children and took part in the three-legged, sack and egg-and-spoon races. I felt a fleeting sadness at the mention of parents, but when I tried to visualise Gloria participating in these childish games, I couldn't.

Us older boys were competitive and took winning much more seriously than the infants, who just saw their races as games. There were lots of different events but the most important race for me was the one I hoped to run in, the relay. I wanted to be part of a team. Each boy had to run a set distance and then pass over a coloured wooden baton to the next boy, who ran on to the next boy and handed over the baton, and so on.

During the games period we practised for all the different races. I was much lighter than the other boys in my class and found that I could outrun them over the short distances. The boys from the orphanage were usually never picked for the games or football teams. We all knew it was because the other children didn't want to mix with us. So even though I knew I was good, I was still surprised when the team leader of the green team picked me and added, 'You're fast, Robbie, you should go last.'

'Last?' I repeated, astonished, for that was the most important position in the team.

'Yes,' he answered. 'We've got to beat the yellow team.'

I nearly jumped up and down in my excitement.

Because an orphanage boy had been picked for the all-important relay team, they were also chattering non-stop about the forthcoming event.

Sports day came at last. It felt like a holiday, as there were no classes. One the way to school we chatted about which races we had entered. For once the rule of silence was lifted and some of the nuns came with us for they wanted to watch the morning's events. Sister Claire held Davie's hand and I heard her ask him what race he was going to compete in. Davie pouted and shook his head in his usual way.

'Not,' he said, followed by 'won't'.

The area around the school gates was crowded as our little crocodile arrived. Instead of saying goodbye to their children, mothers and fathers were walking into the school grounds and onto the playing field, which had a small running track around it. Chairs had been put out for the adults to sit on and tea and biscuits were being served. The races were to start at 10 o'clock. The sun was already beating down and the mothers put their sunhats on. Baby brothers and sisters in prams had the canopies raised and fathers discreetly loosened their ties and placed their jackets on the backs of the chairs.

The Infants' events started first. Little boys ran with outstretched arms, trying to balance a hard-boiled egg on a spoon. The intense concentration on their faces made us all laugh as we stood by and watched. Then it was the mothers' and sons' sack race. Getting down to serious business the participating mothers kicked off their shoes, tucked their flared cotton dresses into the sacks and hopped along beside their little boys towards the starting line.

Sister Claire suddenly jumped up from her seat and grabbed Davie by the hand. 'Come on, Davie, you and I will do this together.' She helped Davie climb into a potato sack and showed him how to hold it tightly so he would not trip and fall over. Then she got into hers, giggling at how her voluminous habit filled it.

The other nuns looked astounded at her actions and I could see them muttering to each other in disapproval. No doubt Sister Bernadette would hear a full report on this disgraceful lapse of dignity, I thought, before straining my eyes to watch my baby brother.

'Ready, steady, go!' shouted the teacher in charge of starting orders. There was utter confusion as the children and their mothers set off. Some fell, some collided and some tripped. Tears followed as pairs of disappointed contestants were disqualified. Davie and Sister Claire were soon in the lead and they jumped determinedly towards the finishing line. She gave a whoop of joy as they crossed the line first. Jumping out of her sack, she swept Davie up in her arms and kissed the top of his head. Davie wrapped his arms around her neck and started to laugh – deep, little-boy belly guffaws. It was the first time I had heard him laugh since the accident. I hoped fervently that it was a sign that he was getting better. Of course, I was still too young to realise that was never going to happen.

Then it was announced that the two relay teams were to gather. The gym teacher spoke into the large metal loudhailer and called us over to take our designated positions. I was the closest to the winning line.

'Just run like hell,' the team's captain said to me as I took my place.

The other team was also from my class and the class above but they wore yellow bibs and we had green ones. The boy who was the last runner for the yellow team and I stood in position, nervously eyeing each other up. He had slicked-back black hair, smart new running shoes and crisp white shorts. Not for the first time, I felt deeply ashamed of my orphanage attire. He jiggled from leg to leg, stretched his arms and legs and looked me up and down as he sneered: 'We'll beat you, you know! Fancy letting a bastard take hold of the last baton!'

Before I could think of a retort the race started. Off the teams went, yellow striding ahead from the start. The batons changed, we caught up. They changed runner again. Neck and neck, the yellow and green bibs ran towards us. We stood ready to grab our batons and run. He got his first; I grasped mine from a panting, red-faced boy, who almost dropped it as he thrust it towards me, and set off as fast as I could. My heart was pounding and my legs were pumping as if my feet weren't quite touching the ground. I loved the feel of the wind gently blowing my hair back as, puffing my chest out, I ran as fast as I could towards the finishing line. He was still in front but something seemed to spur me on. I had a vision of John cheering me from the sidelines; I could imagine hearing him yelling, 'Go, Robbie, go!' And I went.

Slowly I started to gain ground. He could hear my feet pounding up behind him, and when he turned to look an expression of horror crossed his face. That turn did it for me because he lost concentration. It slowed him a fraction and, with John's imaginary voice still ringing in my ears, I pushed forward, touching the winner's tape just inches ahead of him.

The other boys from the orphanage were jumping up and down and screaming with joy. Sister Claire ran over, still holding Davie in her arms. The rest of the green team joined us and I felt hearty pats on the back and words I never expected to hear from my fellow pupils, such as

'Well done, we did it. You did it,' and 'Garner did it for the greens.' This is how it felt to be accepted, to be one of the team, to be a winner and, most of all, to be special again.

'I did it for you, John,' I said quietly, so no one else could hear.

Chapter Twenty-five

As autumn arrived, football became the main topic of conversation and I felt my anger return. Without the physical activity that I had enjoyed in the summer, I felt my anger simmering inside me. It erupted in bad behaviour and I was forever in trouble with the nuns.

I argued with them when reprimanded. I refused to do chores that were asked of me.

'No,' I said several times, 'I won't.'

Once, when I had been out selling flowers from the orphanage gardens, I had been given extra money for myself. I purchased a packet of ten Woodbines and when I returned to Sacre Coeur I lit one in front of the nuns and blew smoke rings in the air above their heads.

Their belts were raised, stinging blows were delivered, but nothing they did could penetrate my angry armour. I never cried when they hit me, never pleaded with them to stop. I just waited for them to finish, then, infusing my stare with as much contempt as possible, locked eyes with them before turning on my heel and sauntering away with my shoulders back and a slight swagger in my walk.

I wasn't to know that they would eventually grow tired of heaping punishments onto me. Neither was I aware that my behaviour was being discussed behind closed doors. I didn't pick up the warning signals of what was to come; there just seemed to be a growing indifference to my many misdeeds. Maybe if I had realised what could happen, I might have tried to curtail my bad behaviour. Instead with the arrogance of a twelve-year-old, almost a teenager, I just thought I was winning.

At school I was different. I worked hard at my lessons and kept my head down. I had ceased to draw attention to myself by always being the first to shoot my hand up in the air and, although that didn't make me more popular, at least the bullying had ended.

In the breaks I hung out with my own group: Marc, Nicolas and Dave, a new boy who had only been in the orphanage a few weeks. Together we presented a united front, although it was Marc and I who were the most disrespectful towards the nuns. Nicolas still had a faint hope, although little remaining belief, that he might be adopted so he tried to behave.

It was surprising that despite our bad behaviour the nuns hired us out as altar boys for weddings and funerals. Maybe the money they received compensated for the fact that it was something that we enjoyed. At the weddings we always felt that we were part of the celebrations and our reward was that we were allowed to consume as much food as we could swallow. If we were lucky, the happy couple sometimes gave us a large-enough portion of the cake for us to take some back and share it with the others.

We didn't like the funerals nearly as much, when we had to stand close to the coffin for hours. But, on the other hand, the food at funerals was often every bit as good as at the weddings. With the to-ing and fro-ing of the mourners it was easy to conceal some of it under our cassocks and smuggle some back to our friends.

In the end it was being altar boys that was Marc's and my undoing.

The two of us were called into Sister Bernadette's office. She informed us that she had decided to bestow what she considered to be a great honour on us.

The old nun from the dining room, who had so often hit us with her ladle, had died. After supper Sister Bernadette told us we were to change into our altar boy regalia and come straight to the dining room. We were to stand vigil over her body.

This was not going to be one of those wakes where we were given plates of good food and sometimes even a tip; it was to mean standing alone in a sparse room with a corpse. But Sister Bernadette was the one nun who could still instil a margin of fear in us so, hiding our dismay at the task ahead, we just answered meekly, 'Yes, Sister.'

Dutifully we changed into our long black cassocks, pulled the white surplices over them, slicked back our hair and went to the nuns' dining room just after they had finished their dinner. Although we had often been in there to clean, that was the first time that we had seen the extent of the food they had for themselves.

The remains of golden-brown roasted chickens, dishes of vegetables covered in thick creamy sauces and tiny Jersey Royal new potatoes, shiny with butter, were still on the table. The polished wooden dining table was almost groaning under the weight of it. On the sideboard was a board where there was not just one cheese but a whole selection of them, from the nearly white Caerphilly to the rich, yellow mature Cheddar. There was home-made crusty bread, plates of biscuits and a large fruit bowl full of oranges, bright red apples and even bunches of grapes.

I felt my mouth water as I stared at all those dishes then thought of the stew we had been given earlier. Almost grey in colour, it contained more greasy fat and bones than meat, and it was served with sprouting old potatoes and overcooked cabbage. I felt a sharp flash of resentment at the nuns' over-indulgence in contrast with their meanness towards us.

Seeing where our gaze was directed, Sister Freda gave a smug little smile, placed her two podgy hands on the table and, with great effort, pushed herself to her feet. Over the years her face had acquired an extra chin or two, whilst her eyes seemed partly obscured by the solid plumpness of her cheeks.

She waddled over to a door leading out of the dining room, imperiously beckoned us to follow and led us into the nuns' quarters. Her breath came in short little puffs as she climbed the steep stairs and took us down gloomy narrow passages that we'd never seen before. At the end of the corridor Sister Freda came to a halt outside a door. She placed her hand on the brass doorknob and turned it.

As we reluctantly stepped into the room, we saw that whatever extravagance the nuns indulged in at the dining table did not extend to their bedrooms. The square, uncarpeted room was painted a stark white. Apart from a wooden crucifix there was nothing, not even a few photographs of the family she surely must have had before she chose a life inside Sacre Coeur's walls. There was nothing to show a glimmer of the character of the woman who had slept in there for so many years – but maybe the very absence of personal belongings had its own message.

There were only five pieces of dark wood furniture in the cold, spartan little room: a desk pushed against a wall, a straight-backed wooden chair tucked half under it, a small chest of drawers, a bedside cabinet with a Bible lying on top, and a single bed. A single bed where the body of the old nun was laid out, dressed in her habit, with a small crucifix and a rosary wedged into her fist.

Sister Freda gave us each a huge candle and lit them, then told us to stand at the foot of the bed.

'It's a big honour for you boys to do this. It will give you a chance to redeem yourselves,' she told us before leaving. The door closed behind her with a click and we stared at each other in horror. Then we stared down at the face of the nun who had terrorised us at so many mealtimes.

Coarse white hairs sprouted from her chin. A bandage was tied firmly round her head to stop her mouth sagging open. Deep lines were etched around her mouth and forehead and the passage of time had cast fine traces of smaller lines on her waxy cheeks, giving them a texture like wrinkled apples that had been stored in a cool place through the winter. Her hands were dotted with a score or more of large brown freckles.

The passing years, which had taken her mind well before we met her, had finally taken what was left of her life. Her mouth, which in life had twisted in rage, would never scream obscenities at us again. The eyes that had glared at us were closed forever, and her gnarled hands that had so often hit us were still, their fingers wrapped round the crucifix and rosary.

In life she had scared me with her volatile temper and propensity to inflict pain, but somehow the still form lying on the small single bed frightened me even more. My teeth started chattering with fear, my hands shook and I saw that Marc looked just as frightened as me. Neither of us had ever been left alone with a dead body before.

Nervous gibberish left our mouths as we both pretended we weren't scared. The shadows deepened as we listened to the distant sounds of the orphanage preparing itself for the end of the day. There were the footsteps of children making their way to bed, the gurgling of old pipes, a faint splashing of water in a drain outside, and the creaks and groans of the old building settling down for the night, and still we stood straining to hear someone approaching the door.

Where was Sister Freda, I wondered? However much we disliked her, that night the sight of her face would have been welcome.

Pins and needles started to prick my legs; I stepped first on one foot then the other to relieve them. My back ached and the candlestick I was holding got heavier by the second. Shadows flickered on the walls, turning Marc's face into a pale mask with dark eyes.

Surely the door would open soon. But it didn't. As the sun went down and lost its warmth, the wind started blowing noisily. A gust of it came through the open window and the curtains lifted as though in the grip of unseen hands. We edged closer to each other. Another gust came, stronger than the last, and extinguished Marc's candle. We were too paralysed with fright to go and switch on a light.

'Surely they can't mean for us to stay in here alone with her all night?' I said.

'Think they do,' Marc answered, his voice quavering.

'Let's do a bunk. I'm not staying here,' I said as bravely as I could.

We measured the short distance to the door in our minds and realised that the corridor outside would be in complete darkness. Suddenly the thought of moving made my body tremble even more than the thought of staying.

Then another question flew into my head: where were the lavatories? No sooner did I think of it than I knew I wanted to go. 'Marc,' I said, 'I need the lav. I'll wet myself otherwise.'

'We're not both supposed to go out of the room at the same time,' he reminded me.

By now my fear of the dead nun outweighed my fear of the living ones. If the idea of wandering down those long dark corridors in the middle of the night terrified me, then the thought that if I went Marc would also want to go when I returned frightened me more. I had no intention of being left alone in that room with the body. I crossed my legs and prayed I could wait.

Gradually our nervous chatter came to an end as we ran out of things to say to each other. The solitary candle flickered, the wind rattled the windows, the pale face of the moon slid behind clouds and even the stars seemed to dim. We tried to avert our gaze from the figure on the bed but over and over our eyes were drawn to her as if mesmerised.

Then, it was as though the old nun, in her final and longest sleep, sensed our presence and felt our fear. We swore later that we saw her move when she played her last trick on us: she belched, with a loud, uncouth sound that vibrated in our ears. We didn't know it was just the air leaving her body. We remembered that the nuns had told us all too often that the dead can rise.

The hairs on the back of my neck stood up, goose pimples rose on my arms, my mouth went dry and my bowels tensed with fear.

'She's … she's come back to haunt us,' Marc said, stuttering with fear and clutching me. 'I want out of here.'

Our eyes darted around. We only had two ways to make our escape: sneaking out through the door into the dark corridors or climbing out the window to the outside.

Without another word Marc and I ran to the window, pushed it fully open and peered down. The gardens had disappeared into the night but darkness was preferable to the eerie shadows of the inside. The nun's room was one floor up but the gymnastics training we had done stood us in good stead. Our eyes met, we gave each other a little grin and a slight nod of the head, then we swung our bodies over the window ledge, seized the drainpipe and, gripping it with our hands and feet, we slid down to the hard surface of the girls' play area.

Chapter Twenty-six

Our knees and knuckles scraped against the wall but we felt only relief at getting away from the dead body that moved and made noises.

On the far side of the girls' area was a path that led to the gates. At that time of night they would be locked so we knew that the only way out was over the wall. We couldn't get to the section of wall that was lowest without going through the building and, apart from the fact that the outer doors were most probably locked, entering the building was not a risk we wanted to take.

'How are we going to get over that wall? It's sharp on the top, you know,' I asked despairingly.

'Sacks from the greenhouses,' said Marc with a grin. 'There's loads of them in there. We'll throw them up, then climb over.'

We ran across the garden and picked up an armful of the coarse sacking.

Never once did we ask each other if we really wanted to climb out; we both accepted that we did. Marc was older and taller than me so he climbed on my back first. He threw up the sacks and used holes in the wall to clamber up to the top. Once he sat astride the wall, with the sacking protecting his bottom, he leant right over, gave me his hand and hauled me up. We looked at the road below and, without another word, dropped down to it.

I don't think at that stage we realised what we had done or gave any real thought to the repercussions of our actions. After the build-up of fear, we were hyped up with excitement.

'Let's get away from here,' Marc said, and I needed no encouragement to take to my heels and run down the road after him as though the devil himself was after us. We didn't stop until we reached Lower Park, over a mile away, where we bent double, rested our hands on our knees and gasped for breath. The wind brought the smell of the sea to our noses and the sound of waves crashing on the nearby beach filled our ears.

'Now what?' I asked, licking my salty lips. A feeling of uneasiness started to fill my adrenalin-fuelled mind. We were so used to being told what to do nearly every minute of the day that some of the elation of being outside those walls was already beginning to wear off.

'Let's get onto the beach,' said Marc and, pushing those feelings aside, I nodded enthusiastically and we set off at a brisk trot. It only took two more minutes to reach the West Park slip, where I breathed in the full force of the salt-tinged air I loved so much. The sea crashing onto the sand had a different sound by night; once the sunlight faded it ceased to be a playground for holidaymakers and turned into a mysterious, watery continent.

We flopped down on the sand, grateful of the rest. I gazed out at the ocean; my memories of an earlier summer on that beach were swirling around in my head. The wind suddenly died down and without its force the dark grey sea, tinged here and there with black and deep-navy shadows, swirled more sluggishly. The white caps of the waves were reflected in the silver light of the moon that had now appeared from behind the clouds. This gave the vast expanse of water an unearthly beauty that the sun's rays seldom gave it in daylight. I decided then that if I ever got away from Jersey I wanted to travel to other continents and explore different oceans and lands.

We had only been there a short time when we became aware of another smell that wafted out from behind a small sand dune: a smoky, spicy aroma that made us feel hungry. We followed our noses until we came to a group of teenagers gathered around a fire where sausages were being grilled.

The beach party, in their shorts and jumpers, stared at us as though we had come from another planet and it was only then we remembered how we were dressed. I suppose two boys wearing black cassocks and white surplices suddenly appearing on the beach at night must have seemed very strange to them.

Marc explained to them what had happened. A combination of looks of amusement at what they thought was our daring escape and expressions of sympathy at our orphaned state appeared on the faces before us.

'Join us,' they said. They were on holiday from England, they told us. A bottle of fizzy drink was put into my hand.

'Fancy a hot dog?' one of the boys asked.

I nodded, not actually knowing what a hot dog was.

Soft white bread rolls filled with hot sausages were passed to us and we shoved them into our mouths with enthusiasm. Pop music, the likes of which we had never heard, played on a small radio that one of the group had brought to the beach. Cigarettes were offered and smoked, more sausages were eaten, and more fizzy drinks were gulped down. The beach was searched for driftwood and the fire was built up again. Around us there were chattering, happy youths, and hearing their laughter we felt warm inside and out. Tiredness overcame us and our eyes shut. Later, we were dimly aware of the group leaving.

'Will you be all right?' they asked us.

'Yeah, we'll have to go back to the orphanage, I suppose,' Marc said, as though it didn't matter.

They looked relieved; after all, what could they have done to help us?

As I heard those words, fear gnawed at my stomach. Although the nuns didn't scare me nearly as much as they had when I was younger, I felt apprehensive as I tried to picture what punishment they would choose to mete out to us for this gross misdeed. We both knew it was too late to try and return before they missed us; anyhow, climbing back in wouldn't be easy. Huddled by the dying embers of the fire, we fell into an uneasy doze. When I awoke the sun had streaked the sky with pink, and Marc was nowhere to be seen.

I pulled my surplice up over my knees, hugged them and gazed out to sea. With the sun's rays already warming the air, it had changed from being a dark mass to a lighter, friendly shade of blue.

'Hey, Robbie, look what I've got!' Marc was back, carrying a greasy paper bag in one hand and a bottle of orange juice in the other.

'Where did you get that?' I asked, when he showed me the hot, crisp bacon rolls in the bag.

'From the Grand Hotel, of course.' Seeing my look of disbelief, he explained that one of the boys he had known in Sacre Coeur now worked there.

'He's given me food before when I've been out selling flowers,' Marc told me.

We tucked into the breakfast and tried not to think of what was going to happen next. Then we brushed ourselves down and decided to head for the town.

That's when we were found.

Chapter Twenty-seven

No sooner had our feet touched the path than we heard the sound of a car engine slowing down.

I felt a trickle of fear slide round my ribs.

'In you get, lads! Fun time's over,' said a gruff voice and, without even looking, we knew it was the police and that it was no good arguing.

Our adventure had ended.

We were placed in the back and two policemen sat in the front. Neither of them spoke to us on that short journey back. They just drove the car through the gates to where Mr Letourneau, the head gardener, was waiting and he took us to Sister Bernadette's office.

As well as being in charge of all the boys given gardening duties, Mr Letourneau was a centenaire, a community policeman. He was the one who had rescued Davie from the broom cupboard the day of his accident and made the nuns take him up to the sick bay. He was a stocky man with lank hair and a weather-beaten face that habitually wore a dour expression and a voice that boomed out orders but seldom made small talk.

That day he drew himself up to his full height, fixed us with a glare and proceeded to lecture us on our misdeeds. He told us that the nuns despaired of us and asked why we didn't appreciate how lucky we were to have had a home with them. Didn't we know that we had let them down and disgraced them and ourselves by this act of defiance? He explained that they were considering what must be done with us.

At that I felt a mounting fear. Was he talking about the mental hospital? I closed my mouth firmly lest I voiced that fear, for if they hadn't thought of it I didn't want to be the one to put the idea in their heads. I saw Marc's face go pale. He had also picked up the barely disguised threat.

Mr Letourneau asked us if we had anything to say in our defence but by that time we were too scared to speak in case we made things worse so we just stared at him, pale-faced and mute.

Sister Bernadette and another nun arrived then. I saw Mr Letourneau shrug his shoulders and heard him tell them that we had not spoken or expressed any shame for what we had done, and then he left, shaking his head in disgust.

The moment the door closed Sister Bernadette's hand swung up then down across my face. Dazed, I fell to the floor. The other nun carried a cane instead of a leather belt. She raised it high in the air and repeatedly brought it down on Marc's shoulders, his back and his bottom. The force of the blows spun him forward, then I heard him scream as he fell to the floor. Blood spurted from a gash on his leg and he curled into a ball trying to protect himself with his hands from the force of the blows. In her fury, she started to beat his arms.

I felt strong fingers in my hair pulling me off the floor until I stood shakily upright. Sister Bernadette's hand crashed down across my face again and I felt blood run from my nose. I knew my lip was cut and I could taste the metallic taste of blood in my mouth and could feel it streaming from my lip and nose. Again I fell. I tried to crawl away. Each blow brought a searing pain far worse than the sting of the leather straps.

The nuns were panting with exertion but they had not finished. They hauled us to our feet and between them pushed and shoved us along the hall towards the boot cupboard. I tried to break away but the other nun holding the cane continued to lash out at both of us with it. Up and down it swished across our exposed legs, arms and shoulders. I saw the muscles in her face contort with such fury that I knew it wasn't just anger she felt but something deeper, a kind of religious fanaticism.

Marc tried not to cry out, tried not to give them that satisfaction, but even he wasn't that brave. And then he started screaming as the attack became more frenzied.

Down and down the cane came, raining indiscriminately on both of us. Like Marc I tried to hold my cries in for as long as possible, but they were not going to stop beating me until I gave in, and through a mist of pain I heard my voice begging them to stop.

They dragged us across the floor to the boot cupboard. We heard the door being opened, felt their feet pushing us, and heard the venom in Sister Bernadette's voice as she hissed, 'You can stay in there without food and think about your sins, you little heathens.'

She left us there for the rest of that day and all of the night. The door was opened briefly for a bucket, a plate of dry bread and a jug of water to be pushed in to us, then it was quickly relocked.

We hurt everywhere. My cut and bruised face throbbed and I knew that the cane had broken the skin elsewhere on my body. My shoulders hurt whenever I leant against the wall, both from the beating and from being roughly dragged and kicked across the floor. It was damp and dark in there and we were cold from shock and hunger. We huddled up to each other for warmth and silently wondered what was going to happen next.

The next day, when we were let out, we met a man called Mr Smith from the welfare department. It was he who told us that the nuns wanted us both transferred to Haut de la Garenne.

To begin with, I was excited. John was there, wasn't he?

On the other hand, the orphanage had become my home, the only one I really knew. It was where my friends and my damaged little brother were.

At the age of twelve, I had spent more time there than I had at Devonshire Place. My memories of that other life before Sacre Coeur were gradually fading, as I'd only been five when I arrived there. At night I tried to picture my family as we had once been, but the tantalising glimpses of my early years had now become insubstantial and vague.

Mr Smith told me I would soon make new friends. I had thought that when I went into the Junior school, but it hadn't happened. I told him about my worries and he pointed out that everyone at the home was in a similar position to me. That reassured me a little.

Mr Smith also told me that life at Haut de la Garenne was much nicer than at the orphanage. 'You'll like it there. I'll tell you something for certain – the food is much better. You don't have to do all of the church stuff or those chores either. After all you'll have more homework, and that's important. Boys like you need to work hard at school and make something of yourselves.'

He then told me that John had left just a short time before, on his fifteenth birthday. He also told me that it was felt at this stage in our lives that it was better that he didn't visit me. The nuns, who seemed to have eyes and ears everywhere, had reported his visits to the staff at Haut de la Garenne. He'd been told that I would be punished if he tried to visit me again.

So that's why he had stopped coming. I felt relieved at the explanation but sad that he wouldn't be at Haut de la Garenne when I got there.

'What about Davie?' I asked Mr Smith. 'Why can't he come as well? He needs me.'

Mr Smith tried to convince me it was best for my younger brother to stay at Sacre Coeur. 'He's better off with the nuns for the moment. He's never going to do well at school, you know.'

I didn't ask him why that was. I suppose I knew, but I didn't want to have it put into words that something had been damaged inside his head, and that he would never recover. At any rate, I failed to understand how staying with the nuns and being separated from me was going to benefit him.

I kept asking every adult I spoke to if Davie could come with me, but they all said 'Not now, Robbie,' and none of them would listen. Their minds were made up.

On the Saturday I was due to leave, Davie was getting ready to work in the gardens. I'd been told that I was to be picked up before lunch and I suddenly realised that this was goodbye. I wanted to delay the moment as long as possible and I kept thinking of excuses to keep him there.

'Robbie, I have to go now,' he said eventually and I heard a faint tremor in his voice.

I looked at the skinny form of my little brother standing in front of me and wanted to hug him, to tell him that everything was going to be all right, that we would meet again. Instead I put my hands in my pockets and swallowed the lump in my throat.

'Davie …' was all I managed to say before my voice dried up completely.

His large blue eyes looked trustingly into mine. He laid a hand on my arm. 'I'll be OK, Robbie,' he said softly. 'It's not for ever, is it?'

'No, Davie, I replied, 'it's not for ever.'

Then he turned and walked out of the dormitory.

Chapter Twenty-eight

'Ready for the off then, Robbie?' boomed Mr Smith's voice. 'Come on, the car's outside. The drive won't take long.'

One hand pushed me gently out of the dormitory, along the familiar corridors, down the stairs and to the front door. Sister Bernadette was there and gave a warm smile to Mr Smith and an inclination of her head towards me.

'Try and behave yourself there, Robbie,' were her final words of goodbye.

I just nodded in reply. If I had hoped for something more, some words saying I would be missed, some sign of caring, even a smile with just a little warmth, then I would have been disappointed. She just stood by the side of the door and watched us walk out. Once outside I took a deep breath and forced a smile. What did I care about Sister Bernadette's indifference to my leaving? I was going to a better place, wasn't I?

I climbed into the front seat of Mr Smith's small black Morris Minor and looked round. The back seat was empty. 'Where's Marc?' I asked. 'I thought he was coming too.' But Mr Smith didn't reply. As the car moved off I gripped the edges of the seat. The engine purred as we travelled out of St Helier and through the countryside towards St Martin.

The drive to Haut de la Garenne passed in a daze. I looked out of the window but took in very little of the view. Too many questions were churning over and over in my head. What was it going to be like there? Would I make friends? Would Davie be all right without me? The couple of times John had visited me, he'd brushed aside my questions and told me very little about the place where he had spent his years in care. I felt another wave of sadness that he was no longer there. It seemed that forces outside our control were determined to keep us apart.

I was brought out of my reverie by the sound of Mr Smith's voice. 'Wake up. Robbie. We're here.'

I looked around me and saw bright green lawns, a large building with freshly painted windows, and I realised that we hadn't driven through huge locked gates. There was no forbidding spike-studded wall surrounding this building and no tribes of little boys digging and hoeing in the gardens.

The head warden was a tall man with a thick bushy beard. He greeted us at the front entrance, shaking Mr Smith warmly by the hand and patting my shoulder.

'Come into my office, Robbie. You and I can have a little chat then I'll get one of the boys to show you around before you have your lunch.' He led the way into a small room with a desk piled high with papers, a filing cabinet and three chairs. He indicated that I was to sit on one of the chairs and took the seat opposite.

He favoured me with a small tight smile, without any of the warmth he had bestowed on Mr Smith, I noticed. He confirmed what I had already been told: that chores were minimal. You just had to make your own bed, keep your sleeping area tidy and take it in turns to help with the washing-up at weekends and in the evenings. That was all.

There was to be no running in the corridors and no raised voices. We had to ask permission of one of the wardens before leaving the premises; just because there were no walls didn't mean we could wander off when we felt like it.

'We caught your brother breaking the rules more than once, you know.' He paused, then gave me a searching look. 'He was very severely punished for that. So we don't want the same behaviour from you, do we?'

I managed to say 'No, sir.' It was news to me that John had been punished and I wondered fearfully what they had done to him.

The other rules were: no fighting, no stealing, no shouting, no answering a warden back and never looking untidy. After what I had been used to with the nuns, it all sounded fairly tame to me.

He told me that disobeying the rules resulted in punishment but he didn't clarify what form the punishment took. Nor did he tell me that it was the individual warden who decided if a boy was untidy or his voice too loud. If I had known then just how they punished us, I might not have felt so confident.

'Now, let's go and find someone who can show you around.'

I followed him out of the office and he called over the first boy he saw. 'Come here, lad.' The boy was snub-nosed with curly brown hair and he looked anxiously in our direction. He seemed very relieved when the head warden introduced us and said, 'Martin will look after you, Robbie,' and disappeared back into his office.

'You're John Garner's kid brother, aren't you?' Martin asked. 'Don't look much alike, do you?' Before I could answer, he carried on chatting. 'We've been expecting you. Heard you were coming.'

'I wish John was still here,' I said sadly. 'I thought he was going to be.'

Martin made no comment to that.

'Come on, let's show you around.' He opened a door. 'This is the dining room.' I was surprised to see that instead of long tables and benches there were big round tables and proper dining chairs. He showed me the cloak-rooms, then the shower areas.

'They're a lot better than baths,' Martin assured me when I confessed that I had never used a shower before. Next he led me down a light, airy corridor where high windows looked over the courtyard and up a flight of stairs and into my dormitory.

'That's your bed,' he said, pointing at a small area where there was a bed, a shiny wooden bedside cabinet and a small wardrobe. I couldn't grasp that all that space was just for me. At the orphanage we hadn't owned anything so there was no need for our own storage area.

'Come on,' Martin said, 'let me take you to the recreation room so you can meet up with some of the others.'

He led the way through freshly painted corridors into a large room furnished with comfortable armchairs drawn up around a black-and-white television set. Floor-to-ceiling bookcases filled with what looked like hundreds of books divided the room and nearly obscured the green-covered table where a group of boys and a dark-haired man in his late thirties were playing a game of pool.

I gaped at my surroundings with open-mouthed amazement. Books, a television and a snooker table! Suddenly the dark rooms and strict regime of the austere orphanage seemed far away. This surely was the start of something better. I began to feel a flutter of excitement. Martin introduced me to two boys who were desultorily playing a game of cards – another pastime that was strictly forbidden in the orphanage. 'Devil's cards', the nuns had called them.

I asked them if they had also known John.

'Everyone knew your brother,' was the answer, followed by the comment that I didn't look at all like him.

I was aware that with my glasses, mousy brown hair and tall, lanky physique, there wasn't even a passing resemblance between my handsome, blond, muscular older brother and me. I did push-ups every day in the hope that my wiry body would turn into a more solid manly shape but it hadn't worked yet.

'Mind you,' said a boy who told me his name was Pete, 'it might be better for you if you don't look too much like him.'

'Why?' I asked. When I saw myself in the mirror and silently compared myself to my elder brother I couldn't think of one good reason why it would be better to look like me.

An uneasy expression crossed Pete's face and a silence descended on our group. I saw their eyes flicker across to where the group of boys and the dark-haired man were playing pool and I felt that somehow my questions had put them all on edge.

'What?' I asked.

'Tell you later, not in here though,' Martin replied quietly, and there was something in the tone of his voice, a warning perhaps, that added a slight tremor of apprehension to my initial excitement.

Keeping their voices right down and glancing at the pool table furtively, they proceeded to fill me in a bit on the wardens.

'The head warden is a right loony,' said a third boy. 'One moment he's all smiles, the next he whams us. You never know with him what way his mood will take him. And that Parker – you'll meet him later – he's another hard bastard. So just keep out of their way.'

The words went straight over my head. Hadn't I been beaten by the nuns for the slightest thing? Hadn't I had to do numerous chores? Hadn't I been denied books, television and games? I looked at the large television that dominated the room and smiled at the prospect of all this freedom.

'When can we watch that?' I asked.

'At weekends when there's a film,' replied Martin without any of the excitement I felt. 'There'll be one this afternoon, most likely.'

Before I could ask any more questions the man who had been playing pool suddenly appeared at my elbow. He told me that his name was Blake and that he was one of the wardens.

In appearance he was cut almost from the same physical cloth as Dennis. Tall and muscular with thick, dark brown, wavy hair and hazel eyes. But as I got to know him better I saw the differences. His eyes didn't crinkle up when he laughed but they changed colour depending on his mood. When they darkened so that they appeared almost brown it was a warning signal to beware of his rising temper. There were other differences as well. Whereas he worked out with dumbbells to keep his body in good shape, sport was not a passion of his – cars were. He had a little red sports model that the boys all wanted to sit in and admire. His walk was different as well; Dennis had been jaunty whereas Blake's was the confident swagger of the predatory bully.

But I didn't see all of that on that first day; I only knew that he made me feel uncomfortable.

He gave me a friendly smile and told me that he was one of the wardens. I felt the boys tense at his presence, and then visibly relax when it was me he addressed. What were they afraid of? My years at Sacre Coeur had taught me never to be disarmed by a pleasant face with a warm smile and not to take encouraging pats on the shoulder or offers of help on trust. At twelve years old I viewed the world and the adults in it with suspicion so I just waited for him to tell me what he wanted.

'You're a lucky boy,' he said. 'There are some nice new clothes waiting for you. Come with me and you can get changed. We need your shoe size then there will be new shoes too.'

He took me back to large cupboard and selected a pair of pyjamas, a dressing gown, a school uniform, and then a pair of trousers and a jumper. My eyes widened at the amount that was there. Carrying the pile of clothing, I followed him up to the dormitory where I put each item in my wardrobe. For the first time since I was five and had been given my new school uniform on the trip to the outfitters, I inhaled the fresh clean smell of new clothes. At the orphanage the combined smell of cheap soap and the staleness of years of use was impregnated into our clothing but these, to me, smelled of fresh air and hope.

'You can put on the trousers and jumper,' Blake said. 'But first you're to take a shower. We can't put clean clothes onto a dirty body now, can we?'

I followed him to a wash area with communal showers. He leant against the wall, watching me as I undressed, and I felt his eyes on me as the water splashed down onto my body. 'Here, let me help you,' he said, and I felt his fingers rubbing shampoo into my hair before running a soapy flannel down my back. I tensed; I didn't like being touched. He noticed and abruptly withdrew his hand.

A towel was thrown round my shoulders.

'Dry yourself with that,' he said.

I turned my back, but all the time I rubbed myself dry I was aware of his eyes on me.

'I expect you're pleased to be away from those nuns,' he said in his deep, gravelly voice, giving me a playful slap across my bare buttocks.

I hurriedly wriggled into my underpants.

'I've heard that they never managed to turn you into a sissy,' he continued.

'No, they didn't,' I said, trying to draw myself up to my full height.

'Yep, heard you were a right little tearaway, just like your brother. Don't try anything on my shift or we won't be friends.'

He gave me a grin, told me it was time for lunch and pointed me in the direction of the dining room.

The next surprise I got was that the dining room was mixed. There were girls there as well. Our table was all boys and Martin had saved a seat for me. When the food arrived my mouth dropped open for the second time that day. Thick slices of ham, fluffy mashed potatoes, peas and carrots; this looked a lot better to me.

We spent most of the afternoon watching a John Wayne Western on the TV and then we had supper: shepherd's pie followed by tinned fruit and custard. After supper we went back to the common room and I tried my hand rather clumsily at a game of pool, and then it was time for bed. I dutifully brushed my teeth, pulled on my new cotton pyjamas, snuggled down under my sheets and blankets and fell asleep with a smile on my face. The hints the boys had dropped about the wardens and the threat of punishment for misdeeds were all forgotten, wiped out by the happy memory of the two good meals, playing pool, seeing a film, a comfortable bed and new clothes. And I was going to meet girls!

This is the place to be, I thought, as I drifted into dreamland.

It was the muffled screams that penetrated my dreams, making my eyes fly open, that changed my mind.

Chapter Twenty-nine

'Go back to sleep,' came a whisper from the boy in the next bed, whose name was Dick. 'You can't do nothing.'

But sleep evaded me. The thick walls might have muffled those screams, but I recognised them as being full of terror and pain. They lasted less than a minute before they were abruptly silenced, and somehow the silence was more terrifying than the screams.

The next morning I asked Dick about them.

'Tell you later,' he said nervously and his eyes darted over my shoulder. I turned around to see what had caught his attention. The warden called Blake was watching us.

I had to wait until after breakfast when we were free to go outside. There was no mass to go to, so even on school days we had this time free. Groups of boys and girls hung around but I noticed that no one seemed to be chatting or laughing.

Martin and I walked out into the sunshine with another boy from my dormitory, who was called Pete. Martin beckoned us to follow him. We finally stopped around the corner where we couldn't be seen from the main building and I could see the boys visibly relax as they leant against the wall. I noticed how alike Pete and Martin were – they could almost be brothers – and I smiled at this thought because John and I hardly looked alike, did we?

Martin spoke first. 'Look, Robbie,' he said, 'it's not a good idea to talk about anything you hear or see in front of the wardens, especially that Blake. There's another one to beware of too, called Parker. Keep your head down and don't draw attention to yourself when either of them are around.' He looked at the ground, avoiding my eyes before asking: 'Did Blake touch you up when he gave you the clothes?'

I shrugged and said, 'Not really,' as nonchalantly as possible. I didn't add that he had made me take a shower in front of him or that there was something about the big, beefy man that made uncomfortable.

Anyhow I wasn't going to let the boys distract me by changing the subject. I wanted to know what had happened in the night. 'Where were those screams coming from?' I asked.

'From the punishment room, near the head warden's office,' Pete told me. 'Usually we can't hear anything but they must have left a door open.'

'The punishment rooms?' I repeated. Just the fact that there were rooms called that gave it a sinister feel and I shivered involuntarily.

The boys looked at each other before Pete continued. 'Don't say anything to anyone. We're not supposed to talk about this, but there are more in the cellars. They're even worse.'

'The one near the head warden's office is mostly used for canings. But they beat you real bad in there,' said Martin with a shudder.

I asked them what happened in the others but they clammed up and it was clear that even talking about it frightened them.

'Who was in that room?' I asked, but as the question left my mouth I felt prickles of apprehension down the back of my neck.

'I think it must have been your friend from Sacre Coeur, that ginger boy – Marc, I think his name is,' Pete said eventually. 'There were no boys from our dorm missing last night.'

'Yes, unusual that, on a Saturday night and all,' muttered Martin. 'Must have been the girls' turn.'

At the time I didn't take in the meaning of his words. I was too shocked to hear Pete saying that it must have been Marc making those dreadful sounds.

I wondered why he hadn't come at the same time as me but just assumed that he would turn up later. Now it seemed that he had arrived and been taken straight to the punishment rooms.

'What could he have done?' I asked.

Martin shrugged. 'Who knows? They don't need you to do anything if they want to beat you; they just do.'

'They're bastards, all of them,' Pete said with a flash of anger in his voice. 'Supposed to be better than us, call us scum, they do. But they are the bleeding scum.' And I saw a sheen of tears mist over his eyes and the anger turned to hatred.

'Maybe he answered the head warden back,' Martin continued. 'That would have done it. Told you he's a mad bastard, that one. Anyway if they want to give you a beating as a sort of welcome to your new home, then they will. If they think a new boy's going to be trouble, that's what they do. Shows them just who's in charge, doesn't it?'

'You two must have been a right handful for the nuns to send you here; we don't get many boys from the orphanage, just the tearaways the nuns can't cope with. Is your friend older than you?' Pete asked.

'Yes,' I replied, 'but only by about six months.'

'Doesn't matter, they'll assume he's the ringleader then, so it's him they'll go for first. Whop any spirit out of him. That's what they try and do.'

I left it at that. I was worried about Marc, sorry that he had taken a punishment for both our misdeeds, if that was the case, and petrified that one day I would be taken up to that punishment room. With my shoulders hunched I walked back into the common room, took down a book and sat in a chair away from the groups of boys who were chatting quietly amongst themselves. I turned the pages but my eyes and brain were unconnected. I didn't take in a word. I tried to empty my mind of all the thoughts that raced around in it and the day seemed to pass without my awareness of anything around me.

But that night, when I lay in my bed, the one thought that kept repeating itself over and over in my mind was: I've come to somewhere worse. What I didn't know then was just how much worse it was.

They released Marc the next morning – a Marc I hardly recognised. It was just two days since I had seen him last but he looked older and thinner. I knew he was badly bruised; I could tell by the way he was holding himself. His arms were wrapped around his body as though to protect it from further blows.

His eyes met mine and I saw that there was no trace of childhood naivety or trust left: instead there was a blank deadness. It was a look I came to recognise, a look that settles in the eyes of the young when all hope and all belief that life will get better have gone. The boy who had brought us food and reassured me that Davie was all right when I was locked in the chicken sheds, the boy who had made my days working in the laundry bearable and had laughed with me on that beach just days before, had gone; in his place a hurt, bewildered shell remained.

He said nothing for a few seconds, and then sighed. 'They're bastards, Robbie; real bastards.' And as he uttered those words I saw to my horror that one of his upper front teeth was missing.

'Marc,' I said, then my words dried up and I just stood there looking at him, my arms dangling uselessly at my sides. I wanted to comfort him as he had once comforted me, but I was too young to know the words to express what I felt, so I said nothing.

Later, in a secluded area of the grounds, he pulled his shirt up and showed me his bruises. His ribs were mottled and there were livid marks on his back. There were also bruises that had clearly been caused by a clenched fist and others raised into weals that he said were cane marks.

'But there are ones you can't see,' he said grimly. 'Those bastards have ways of hurting you where it doesn't show. They roll up something hard in a wet towel then they beat you with it.'

'I heard you screaming,' I said eventually. I thought for a moment and remembered that even when he was eight he had never screamed when the nuns beat him.

He didn't tell me then what had made him cry out and beg them to stop. I put the story together over the next few days as he told me little scraps of what they had done to him.

Three men had taken him down to the cellars, stripped him and put him into a bath filled with icy cold water. They held his head under so long that he thought he was drowning. Then they brought him back upstairs and beat him. They threatened him with the icy bath again and started dragging him to the door, punching him on the back.

If that hadn't made him scream, what had? I wondered. I needed to know what had happened to Marc and what could lie in wait for me if I didn't toe the line in this place.

It was later that day when he told me the rest. We had taken ourselves to a sheltered part of the grounds, where we thought we would be unobserved from the main building. The wardens didn't seem interested in keeping us apart even though Marc had been put in a different dormitory from me. I suppose they thought that after Marc's punishment we'd had enough of a warning. We were sitting on the lawn, both deep in thought about his ordeal. As though reading my mind, he finally had the courage to answer my silent question.

'They put things on my willy,' he said suddenly. 'Things that hurt.'

I was listening so hard I could hardly breathe. A tear rolled down his face. He wiped it angrily away with the cuff of his shirt. 'It was that that made me scream, Robbie. I couldn't help it.'

He got up off the grass and walked away, his shoulders hunched and his hands deep in his pockets. I sensed that he didn't want me to follow him.

At the time I couldn't imagine what he meant. What could they have put on his willy? Over the next few days I worked it out, partly from what Marc told me, partly from what I managed to get out of Martin and Pete.

The wardens kept a small generator locked up in the cellar. They had switched it on when they took Marc down there the second time. They showed it to him; let him know it was electric. He knew that electricity and water mixed together could kill you and he started to shake with terror. They laughed at his fear and picked up the metal probe they had attached to the generator. It was the sort that farmers use to stun cows before they're killed.

He had seen them used on the dairy farm where he had once lived when he was little. They touched his genitals with it. The pain was so intense it would have made a grown man scream. Marc was still only thirteen. It was a torture that, once used, had even the bravest boys reduced to a shivering jelly at the very sight of it.

It was then he had screamed and screamed, sobbed uncontrollably and begged them not to do it again. When they had brought him upstairs he thought that they were going to let him go at last, but that was just another way of tormenting him. They knocked him about some more, then, when he was on the floor, they grabbed his legs and started dragging him towards the door.

They threatened him with that probe again, that and the cold bath. His body had writhed and jerked with remembered pain, his hands had reached for the door jamb and gripped it so hard he broke his nails. They just laughed and kicked him again. He screamed as he had in the cellar and begged them not to take him back there. It was these screams we had heard as we lay in the dormitory.

Satisfied that they had broken his spirit, they didn't torture him any more after that. They just left him in a room where there was only a thin mattress to lie on and nothing to keep him warm. He was in shock from the beatings, his body chilled by the cold water, and he was still twitching from the remembered agony of the electric shock. He spent that night shaking and crying with the cold and his pain.

In the morning when they had come for him he had promised to be good.

He hated himself for crying.

He hated them.

Even between ourselves we rarely admitted that we were scared. Shame kept us quiet. Shame of our fear, at what the wardens could, and did, do to us. Shame at how they reduced us to what we thought of as pitiful objects and how they had made us cry and beg.

We all knew that there was no use asking for help from people outside the home. We were there because we were unwanted. We were all there for a reason. Some boys had committed crimes and were considered too young for prison; others were abandoned; some had a single parent who had become ill and could no longer look after them; and some had learning difficulties or personality disorders and had been placed there by a family who didn't want them or couldn't handle them. Everyone knew we were problem children. We had all at various times been told we were useless, failures and scum. The head warden and his team were respected citizens; they helped keep Jersey's streets free of troublesome youths. They knew people in high places; they told us no one would ever believe us. They would just say we made up wicked stories. The only people our stories would harm would be ourselves.

Then there was the threat that had followed us from Sacre Coeur – the mental hospital. Boys who were not believed were clearly compulsive liars. Liars were either sick or bad. The sorts of stories we had to tell were so dreadful we might qualify on both counts. Sick enough to go to the hospital, be locked up with the loonies and have to stay there at the mercy of doctors who might decide never to release us into the world.

At least we knew that, in the home, reaching the age of fifteen would bring us freedom.

Chapter Thirty

During my first few days at Haut de la Garenne, I could sense that there was something about my brother that Pete and Martin were not telling me. 'Was he popular?' I asked, trying to draw them out.

'Oh yes,' Martin said. 'Everyone liked John. Didn't they, Pete?'

Pete nodded in agreement but still I sensed that my brother and his experiences here were not a topic they wanted to discuss.

'What is it then? There's something you're not telling me.'

Pete looked at Martin, who shrugged and said, 'Oh, go ahead, we might as well tell him. He'll find out anyhow.'

Martin began: 'Pete knew him better than me, he was already here when your brother first arrived, but I know John was given a hard time.'

'Yeah, that's right,' continued Pete. 'The bastard wardens seemed to have it in for him as soon as he walked through those doors. Don't know how he's still OK. But I'll tell you something he said to me once. I've never forgotten it, Robbie.' He looked at me intently. 'He said he had to be strong 'cos one day he, you and that other brother of yours were going to be together again and 'cos he's the eldest it was up to him to take responsibility for making it happen. And I reckon that despite all they did to him, that's what kept him right in the head.'

I felt a lump in my throat and my eyes prickled with emotion. I could just hear John saying that, even back at the age of eight. After all, it had been up to him to look after us almost from the day we were born.

I waited for him to continue and, seeing that I wasn't going to be satisfied until I knew everything, he sighed and reluctantly started telling me about the years John had spent in Haut de la Garenne.

John might have been my big brother, my hero when I was only five and he was eight, but now that I was twelve I realised that he was really only a little boy when we had been separated. I had at least had Davie, but he had no one. John had been such a beautiful little boy – one who walked like a bigger boy, because that was what life had demanded of him.

But at night he wet the bed, which was a punishable offence in Haut de la Garenne.

'Parker had just started here then. Remember I told you he's a real evil bugger, that one?' Pete said. 'John was scared all right. Poor little sod tried to make the bed without anyone knowing. He put something under the sheet, you know, to stop it staining the mattress. He got away with it for a couple of days but it whiffed a bit and someone told Parker. He came into the dormitory early the next morning and pulled John out of bed. Sure enough, he had done it again. Parker told all the boys in the dorm to stay and watch what happens to dirty little sods like John. I was in the bed opposite him, so I could hear and see everything.'

I felt an icy coldness in the pit of my stomach at the thought of John's shame that morning when he had been pulled out of bed and shown up in front of the thirty boys who slept in that dormitory. I remembered when I had helped him hide the sheets from Gloria and imagined how upset and frightened he must have been without me to help.

'What happened then?' I asked. I was finding it hard to hear these things, but I needed to know.

Pete furrowed his brow in concentration and I knew he was picturing my brother as he had been that morning.

'Parker shouted at him, called him a dirty little bleeder. John just looked up at him with those big grey eyes of his. Didn't cry, just stood there. Then Parker made him take off his pyjamas. Told him they needed washing, and when he was standing there naked Parker made him strip the bed. John was bright red by then and still that bastard hadn't finished with him. He put the sheet over John's shoulders and head and pulled the wet bit around his face. "Now smell your own piss," he shouted at him, playing to the audience of us boys as well. And still your brother didn't cry, and that's what made Parker really mad. He grabbed John and pushed him towards the door and yelled at all of us to get down to the playing fields. He even told one of the boys to go to the other dormitories and tell them he wanted everyone outside as well.'

I closed my eyes and squeezed back the hot tears that threatened to run down my cheek at the image Pete had conjured up. I could hardly bear to think of that proud little boy being so humiliated by strangers. Pete's story continued and I wanted to put my hands over my ears to block out the words, but I didn't.

'Parker made him run round the grounds naked with his wet sheet on his head and made the rest of us watch him. He told them all what John had done and called him the little pisser. Some of the boys laughed and jeered but others were frightened. Parker was so scary then, even more than he is now. I wasn't even six when it happened, but it's something I remember very vividly. I used to wet the bed when I was little and it scared me that this could also happen to me. But John still didn't cry, you know. Not then.'

'What did Parker do after that?' I knew that no amount of humiliating punishment could make a person stop bed-wetting.

'Oh, Parker often made him do it. We all got used to seeing John running with that sheet over his head. Didn't matter what the weather was like, Parker made him run. And then your brother got his own back; he got the better of Parker. Of course that meant that Parker really hated him then, but I think John thought it was worth it.'

I heard the note of admiration in his voice. 'How?' I asked. 'How did he do that?'

'It was only a few weeks after he had come here,' Pete continued. 'I think John had worked Parker out. Anyhow, he got up before Parker came in the morning, washed the piss out of the sheet and then stood by his bed waiting. When Parker came into the dorm John said he was ready for his run. And do you know what he did when he got onto the grass?' I shook my head and Pete answered himself. 'He took that sheet, waved it above his head and ran so fast that the boys started cheering him on. John laughed, raised his other hand and waved. He looked just like an Olympic runner crossing the winner's line! Parker was purple with anger and he really had it in for John after that. But that was your brother all right, he really was the dog's bollocks. Even the older boys admired him.'

I pictured John as he would have been then, with his white-blond hair, pale-golden skin and compact little body, pumping his legs furiously as he ran faster and faster with the sheet billowing above his head like a giant victory flag. I saw his grin, that wide 'I don't care' grin of his, and I felt a surge of pride for the plucky eight-year-old he had been.

Pete told me that after that Parker became determined to break John's spirit, and any misdeed, no matter how tiny, was picked on and punished. 'If he was walking too fast he was accused of running, too slow then he was dawdling, and when he tried to defend himself, arguing with authority and being cheeky. I remember the first time he was caned. They did it in front of us in the dormitory. Parker pulled his trousers down, made him lean over the bed and told him to spread his legs. He used the woopy cane on him,' he said, using the nickname for a cane that made a fierce swishing sound when brought down swiftly onto bare flesh. Its ends were split and sharp enough to draw blood. I'd heard about these from some boys at Sacre Coeur, even though the nuns never used anything like this, and I cringed inwardly at the thought of that type of cane being used on eight-year-old John's delicate skin.

'He belted John with that cane good and proper. His arse was fire-engine red and cut so bad he was bleeding all over the place. John cried; he tried hard not to but he couldn't help it. He was black and blue for the whole week after. That was the only time I saw him cry, though; he was no coward, he always kept his head up.'

Pete went silent and clenched his fists with the effort of finding the words to tell me more.

'It was those men, those filthy scum bags,' he spat the words out with a sudden, fierce anger. 'You know those bastards that always want to feel us up? They really hurt him bad.' Pete's hand went up to his mouth, almost as though he wanted to push back the words. 'He fought them, but he was only about nine then. He cussed them out anyhow he knew and kicked and spat at them. He just wasn't having any of it.'

Pete looked miserable remembering. 'It's wicked,' he said. 'They're wicked. He got whopped a lot. It must have been when he'd been in here for about two years that it got even worse. He bit one of the wardens' hands, didn't like where the bastard had been trying to put it! They took him down to the cellars and beat him. Anyhow, Robbie, I don't know for a fact what went on there 'cos I wasn't down there with him, but there was blood on his underpants, I saw that all right the next day. And he walked really funny, you know as if he was really hurt. We asked, but he didn't talk about it. He wouldn't, no matter how hard we tried. He only got angry if anyone asked. I was about eight then and I sort of knew what had happened. I'd been touched – you know, had my willy pulled – and had been made to hold one of those men's, but that was all. So I didn't really know but I knew it was bad, knew they had hurt him.'

I felt sick. I wanted to beg Pete to stop. To tell him that I didn't want to hear any more, that I couldn't cope with it. But I didn't. Maybe in a way I felt I owed it to John to listen to the rest.

Pete's eyes darted round almost fearfully, checking that there was no one in earshot. 'You see that warden, Blake? He likes young boys, that one. Things got even worse when he came because he wanted your brother for himself. John was forever being taken down to the cellars. Anyhow, when he got a bit bigger he hit Blake. Didn't see it, wished I had, but there were other boys down there. It was at one of their "parties". John drew back his fist and hit Blake right in the mouth. Called him a bleeding poofter and all.'

I wondered what they meant by 'parties' but didn't like to ask.

Martin spoke then. 'Yeah, that was when I was here. Those bastards beat him up so badly he was kept down in those rooms in the cellar for two days. They had him in the room with the bath. It was Blake himself, the sick fucking bastard. When he was good and sloshed, he bragged about what they did to him. He was laughing his stupid head off too; he wanted us to know what happens to anyone who dares to lift a hand to one of them.

'Anyway, they put a sort of hood over his head, put him in the bath and held his head under. There's no one who wouldn't panic when that hood's over your face and your head is under water. It's like drowning. Your brother would have thrashed and thrashed, heard their laughter and thought he was dying. Maybe hoped he was.' His voice dropped so low that the next words were almost whispered. 'They did it to me once too.'

He had averted his eyes while relating this bit, but on finishing he lifted his head to see if I was coping with everything he'd told me. I looked back at him through a film of tears. All of a sudden Martin looked like a defeated, hunched-up old man who had reached the end of his life, not a thirteen-year-old boy who should have had everything to look forward to.

'You'd do anything for them not to do that to you again.'

The chill in my stomach turned to ice. I thought of the times John had managed to sneak out and see me and hadn't said a word about what they did to him in this place.

'Anyhow,' Pete continued a bit more cheerfully, 'by the time he was coming up to leave here things got better for him. I don't know, but I think Blake started getting scared of him. Your brother might have been only fourteen but he was pretty big and muscular, what with the gym training and all. You know he did push-ups and lifted some sort of weights? Every spare moment he had, we would see him running round and round the grounds. Don't know where he got the weights from but he used them every morning before the wardens came in. I could barely lift those weights and he did it like they were plastic. He told us he was training, but he never said what he was training for.' He looked thoughtful. 'Yes, I think Blake was pleased when he finally left, all right.'

I remembered admiring John's athletic physique when he had visited me at Sacre Coeur. He'd had broad shoulders, a slim waist and clearly defined muscles in his arms and legs.

Now I knew why he had made himself so muscular: he'd done it in order to survive.

Chapter Thirty-one

All my life I had envied John his good looks. While he had thick, white-blond hair, mine was an unprepossessing mouse colour and so fine it flopped limply across my forehead. Long, almost black eyelashes framed John's light-grey eyes set under darker blond brows, while my washed-out murky-blue eyes peered at the world through pale-pink plastic frames. John's skin always appeared slightly tanned and was clear of the teenage spots that plagued his contemporaries and that I was expecting to erupt on my face any day now.

In contrast to his muscular build, my shoulders were narrow and my arms and legs were skin and bone. I was still trying to do press-ups every day but there didn't appear to be any sudden spurt in muscle growth and I despaired that, try as I may, I would never look like John when I was fully grown.

But by the time I had been in Haut de la Garenne for a few days, I was grateful that I didn't have my brother's good looks. It didn't take me long to learn the advantages of not having the label 'pretty boy' attached to me, for I often heard sobs and muffled pleas in the dorm at night and I realised that they mostly came from one of them.

When I was woken by soft, stealthy footsteps creeping across the dormitory floor, I held my breath to try and silence my breathing. We all did, every one of us in that room. We didn't want to do the slightest thing that would draw attention to us. We lay there, our bodies curled up tightly in our beds and our fear palpable, waiting for the footsteps to stop by the bed of one small, hunched-up figure. We prayed that it was not going to be our bed that those large men, into whose care we had been entrusted, stopped at. 'Anyone else, please God,' I prayed, 'anyone else who isn't me.'

We squeezed our eyes tightly shut one moment and then, desperate to know if they had already passed us by, we peered out between our lashes the next. We saw through half-closed eyes which beds they went to. There were three boys in our dormitory who were taken on a regular basis. But any pity I felt for those chosen boys was by far outweighed by my relief that it wasn't me. At least, not this time.

I knew without seeing them that those boys' knuckles would be white with their futile efforts at resistance. Small hands clutching the edge of the mattress as hard as they could were no defence against brawny men deter-mined to wrench them from their bed. Those nights, while I lay in my bed pretending to be asleep, I heard when an adult's hand covered a small boy's mouth. I heard the gasp abruptly cut off, the sound of bare feet scrabbling on the floor and knew that the boy had been pulled from his bed and was being dragged from the room. I thought of the fear he must be feeling, of the tears that would be running down his face. I knew the words that would be spinning around and around in that petrified boy's mind. 'Stop them, somebody please stop them. Help me!' But nobody ever did.

With their departure I could hear the faint sound of released breath and the tiny movements of bunched-up muscles relaxing. Every time it happened I was sure I could smell the faint whiff of a little boy's pee that had dampened the sheets of an empty bed.

Yes, we all knew what was happening. But we were only children who were far too controlled by fear to find the guts to leap to one another's defence.

We all knew that their journey would take them to the cellars where someone would be waiting. Sometimes another warden or maybe a man from outside.

There was one man who visited us regularly, walked down the long corridors freely, laughed and joked with the wardens and at Christmas time, while 'Jingle Bells' played on the radio in the common room, he gave small children brightly wrapped presents, sweets and jovial smiles as he sat them on his knee.

To the boys who were brought to him in the cellars at night, where he crouched in the shadows waiting for them to be delivered, he gave something else – something special, he told them. He gave them pain and shame.

When the hand was removed from a boy's mouth I would hear faint cries and pleas disappearing down the corridor and, unable to bear those sounds, I put my hands over my ears. In the dining room the following morning I averted my eyes from the pale faces of the chosen boys and if there was an empty place I didn't ask where the missing boy was.

The small group we called 'the pretty boys' all clung together. Both their shame at being taken night after night and ours at not helping them kept them separate from us.

Sometimes I would see them in the corridors walking ahead of me. They would flinch when a warden or a group of older boys approached them, for it was not just the wardens who bullied them. There was a gang who lay in wait for the pretty boys, and my group knew to stay well clear of them.

These were boys who had got into trouble on the outside, fighting, stealing and playing truant. Rejected by their natural parents and handed back by foster parents when small and cute became large, sullen and aggressive as their teenage hormones kicked in, they were the ones who entered the home with acne on their faces and large chips on their shoulders.

They took pride in their poor school marks, showed little interest in team games, cleaned their fingernails with penknives, avoided washing, smoked in corners and Brylcreemed their greasy hair. They found each other in the home and created their own little gangs who used their fists and feet and made catapults which fired stinging missiles. They laughed when their victims jumped, winced and cringed.

No doubt once upon a time they had been bullied, called little bastards, tripped up and jeered at themselves. Over the years they had made the transition from being helpless little boys to being young thugs without a great deal of effort. They saw violence and cruelty as the norm.

The worst of them was a slack-mouthed boy who had been given the nickname Spud. His intelligence was so low he couldn't work out why his round pasty face, short thick neck, bristly sandy-coloured hair and small mean eyes had earned him that name. By the time I met him, nobody dared tell him.

He formed his own group of like-minded dullards with two other boys who were brothers. They stalked the younger children and became the wardens' accomplices, for even they did not want to mess with this trio of feral boys.

One of Spud's favourite daytime games was to stake out the lavatories and wash areas. He would lie in wait until an unsuspecting boy bent over the sink to brush his teeth or wash his face. With a leer, Spud would creep towards him, place his large meaty hands on either side of his victim and rest them against the sink, holding the boy firmly in place. His eyes would close to slits and his mouth drool as he jerked himself back and forth against the boy's buttocks.

Lonely corridors were unsafe places so I always hurried along them as quickly as I could. However, one

day a few weeks after I arrived I saw Blake's tall, thickset
body coming towards me with that self-confident swagger that defied anyone to challenge him. A wide, mocking smile was plastered across his face.

'Go past me,' I begged him silently, as I tried to look
anywhere but at him. But he didn't.

'Hey, Robbie,' he said as though we were friends,
'there's a party tonight and you're invited.'

I looked up at the man, who in a few short weeks I had
already learnt to distrust, and I'm sure my face registered
my suspicion. Pete and Martin had mentioned 'parties'
and although they hadn't explained exactly what they
were I knew I didn't like the sound of them.

He ignored my expression and carried on: 'Just an inti-
mate little get-together so we can all become better
acquainted. You know, learn about each other a bit more.'

'Who else is coming then?' I managed to ask, seeing no
alternative but to play along with his game.

'A few of you lads, a couple of my friends and Anderson,' he replied. At the sound of Anderson's name, I felt a
wave of fear. He was another warden and one of the men
who came to the dormitories in the night.

I thought of Neville then, those fat fingers prodding at
my small body, the heat of him through my jumper, the
way my small hands had been forced to stroke him, and
afterwards that smell – that smell when his slime stuck to
my fingers.

I remembered how when I had first known Dennis I
had seen him as someone to look up to and admire. I had

been so happy, so flattered and so excited when he picked me for the gymnastics team that I had found it difficult to sleep the night after he had told me. But I had quickly learnt that an apparently kind smile could disguise a very different kind of man. A picture flashed into my mind of him naked, sitting with his legs spread wide, playing with his penis as though it was a pet rat, and I shuddered.

But bad as those two had been, I knew this would probably be worse. I remembered the unease I had felt when Blake watched me taking my first-ever shower on the day I arrived at Haut de le Garenne.

I opened my mouth to say no. No, I didn't want to go to the party, especially if they were going to be there.

He forestalled me. I was not going to get a chance to refuse. His hand gripped my wrist in a powerful hold.

'After supper you go to your dormitory and wait for us. All right?'

I felt the chill of fear in my stomach. I just looked at him. What could I say?

'Don't worry if you're shy, Garner,' he said in a tone that was meant to be reassuring but that frightened me even more. 'You'll soon know us well. So you will be ready, won't you?'

I knew that this wasn't something I had a choice about and that to ignore his command would bring down unimaginable repercussions on my shoulders. I swallowed hard. I felt sick. I'd hoped that maybe I had escaped his notice but I realised that he had just been playing for time.

I wanted to escape, to run from him, but there was nowhere or nobody to run to.

'Yes,' I said.

He smiled again, patted me just a little too heavily on the bottom, and strode off. His mouth was pursed in a tuneless whistle, his arms swinging; he was a man looking forward to the evening ahead.

There were six of us waiting by our beds that night, six of us who did not want to meet each other's eyes, six of us who already felt ashamed of something that had not yet taken place.

Chapter Thirty-two

We didn't have long to wait before we heard heavy footsteps walking along the corridor. There was the murmur of a deep male voice and another chuckling in reply, and then they were in the dormitory. The bulky Blake, with the smile that chilled me, was with his friend Parker, a wiry, sandy-haired warden who I would guess was somewhere in his thirties, maybe slightly younger than Blake.

'Good boys!' Blake said heartily, continuing with the charade that we were willing participants in his game. 'I can see you're all looking forward to some fun.'

Both men rubbed their hands together as though they were cold and we were all being so quiet that the papery sound their palms made seemed loud. Our senses were on high alert.

Parker said nothing, just stood a little behind Blake eyeing us each up and down. I felt the heat of his gaze and felt defiled by it. He cracked his hairy knuckles, a popping sound that sliced into the silence.

Blake moved closer to me, put his hand under my chin and raised it so that his eyes met mine. His breath was tainted with the odour of stale cigarettes, beer and feral expectation. It soured the air that I inhaled and for a few seconds I tried to hold my breath. My nose twitched with distaste and I felt completely trapped by his closeness, for my locker was behind me and my bed was to my side. I could see his eyes were glistening brightly with anticipation.

'Come on, boys,' both Parker and Blake said in unison. 'The party's about to start!' added Blake.

Heavy arms were thrown over skinny shoulders, encouraging smiles given by moist lips; just the force of their presence propelled us out of the security of our dormitory. Not one of us boys came higher than their broad chests and we were all so slight that had we been placed behind them no one would have been able to see us. Down the corridor we went. Trying to think of anything but what was to come, I reflected that over my short life I must have walked many miles along narrow passages and dark corridors. All those miles that had so often led me to places I didn't want to go to.

That night it was my footsteps I could hear ringing in my ears. We didn't pass anyone else on that walk to the cellar door. It was as though some sort of common consent cleared the corridors for us to walk through unobserved. I wondered if there were other boys hidden behind doors, grateful it wasn't them who were being taken.

Broad stairs led to the hallway, then a door was opened and we had to climb in single file down a steep flight of stairs, the ones that led to the cellars. A single lightbulb illuminated the part of the underground room we came into and candles threw shadows into nooks and alcoves. In contrast to the freshly painted rooms in the rest of the building, the basement had a musty, dank smell. There were large dark patches where plaster had flaked off the walls, and under our feet was rough cement and brick.

We could hear laughter echoing along the passages and it sounded as though it came from far away. I felt the heaviness of Blake's arm and heard his voice in my ear: 'We're here, Robbie.'

A dim light was glowing under a door. The faint hope that I was just having a bad dream, and that at any moment I would open my eyes and find myself in the common room with my friends or even getting ready for bed, disappeared. That door was where the laughter was coming from and that room was where the party was being held.

Another door was opened and we were pushed inside. Blake struck a match and lit a candle. We were in a small, dark room that was unfurnished apart from a thin mattress. I blinked, my eyes trying to see in the gloom, and I saw Blake bend to pick something up off the floor and push it into my arms. I looked down. It seemed to me like pieces of clothing.

'I forgot to tell you it's a fancy-dress do,' he laughed, and that laugh added to my already-high anxiety levels.

'This is your changing room, boys. I want you out of those clothes and into the ones we've given you; something that will suit you. You've got five minutes. I want every piece of your clothing off before you put on your costumes.'

He handed the others their costumes for the evening and then his gaze shifted back to me.

'Robbie, you're new. I don't want you making any mistakes because we don't want the other guests getting angry, do we? So I'll repeat myself for your benefit. I said "every" piece of clothing. Do you understand me?' My face burned with shame. I knew he was waiting for an answer.

'Yes, I understand,' I replied.

I heard his mocking voice again: 'That means your glasses as well. You'll be able to see all you need to see without them.' He laughed as though he had cracked a very funny joke, but it was one that only he could understand.

Bored with tormenting me, Blake turned to one of the other two, a ten-year-old boy called Christopher, who I recognised as being one of the boys who was 'taken' regularly. He usually hung out with the sad little group of pretty boys. Even within that group his ethereal beauty made him stand out. With his pale creamy skin, deep pink lips, wide brown eyes and his mass of dark brown curls shot through with gold, he reminded me of a picture of an angel that I had seen at the orphanage. Amidst the horrors of the crucifixion that hung on most of the walls there, it was one of the very few images that I had liked. Sister Claire had explained, when I remarked on it, that the original painting had been done a very long time ago and that the artist's name was Botticelli.

Blake leant closer to the pretty boy, ran his index finger up and down the slender neck, drew it across the boy's cheeks in a mockery of a caress and brushed his lips, which trembled in response. He leant even closer and whispered something that I couldn't hear. The slim shoulders flinched and even in the dim candlelight I could see a deep blush staining the boy's cheeks.

Blake said to him, 'I hope you're going to like your costume. I chose it especially for you, Chrissie boy.' Christopher just hung his head; his lips moved in reply but his mouthed words were totally indistinguishable.

The candlelight flickered over our pale bodies as we changed. Skinny legs stepped out of trousers, jumpers were pulled up and over drooping heads, shoes were tugged off and socks slowly rolled down and removed until there were six little piles of reluctantly discarded clothing. I glanced at my companions as we changed. No one spoke. I wanted to ask the other boys what happened next, but I couldn't summon up the words.

I later discovered that all the other boys, apart from the youngest, had been to the cellars before and they already knew what would happen. We were the toys; toys that came in different sizes, toys for grown men to play with.

I heard Christopher give a gasp that was almost a groan as he unrolled his costume. I couldn't see what it was, only that it looked white and very sparkly.

I picked mine up from the floor where I had placed it when I undressed. At first glance it didn't appear too bad, like a long cloak with a hood. There was something hard concealed in the folds and when I unwrapped it I saw what at first looked like an innocent lump of plastic that was such a pale pink it seemed almost white. I looked at it curiously. I saw it had straps attached to it and it was then I realized it was part of my costume.

Suddenly there was something repellent about that lump of plastic. I knew I didn't want to touch it. I certainly knew I didn't want to wear it, even if I had understood where it was to go. It was only a thing, I told myself as I tried to calm my racing mind; only a thing.

The boy nearest to me was pulling on a Tarzan costume, an imitation fur cloth that fastened over one shoulder and barely fell to crutch level. He had his back to me and I noticed he kept pulling it down as far as it would go in an attempt to cover his bottom. His name was Matt and I knew that he hadn't been in the home long. I'd heard that his mother couldn't control him and that he got into frequent fights. Up until that night, I had tried to avoid him. He was a boy who scowled more than he smiled and whose clenched fists held stiffly at his side always made him look as though he was spoiling for a fight. But that night he didn't look ready for an altercation; he looked like the miserable, scared nine-year-old he was. Without his trousers and jumper I could see the yellow marks of old bruises covering most of his ribs, and some circular brown scars that I guessed must have been caused by burns from a lit cigarette.

'Matt,' I whispered. 'What's this?' I pointed to the plastic lump.

'It's your hump, Robbie. These bastards like that one all right,' he replied, as though I should know what it meant. Seeing that I still hadn't caught on, he gave me a

pitying look. 'It's the hunchback's costume; you know –
the one they made a film about.'

I winced, for I knew that story; it was a vivid memory
from my time in the orphanage, where it was one of the
few films the nuns had let us watch. For some reason,
maybe because it was set in Paris's Notre Dame Cathedral
and Quasimodo, the hideously deformed hunchback, had
been a bellringer, they had decided it was educational.
Victor Hugo's book, which the film was based on, was
considered a literary classic, and they admired education.

I had only been six when the nuns sat us down in front
of an old black-and-white television and told us all to be
very quiet. It was an event so rare that in all the years I
was at Sacre Coeur I only watched that television twice.
On the screen I had seen a beautiful gypsy girl with long,
thick, curly hair and a man so hideously ugly and
deformed that he made me shiver with horror.

The dramatic contrast with her daintiness made the
bellringer even more revolting and I was far too young to
realise how much of that ugliness was down to make-up
and stage props. At that age I just found him sickeningly
repulsive.

I wondered why they would want me to wear something that made me look deformed.

Matt looked almost sorry for me then. 'I'll give you a
hand. Buggers put it on me first time they dragged me
down here; it's the initiation one,' he said.

He helped me fasten it so that the dreadful pink hump
was in the centre of my back.

He noticed me looking at his burn marks and said, 'My stepdad did these. And you know what? My bleeding mum, she just watched him do it. Said I had to be taught a lesson because I was always being bad. He knocked me about too. I don't know who told, but someone from the welfare came and they put me here. They don't know this place is even worse.' He didn't say who had given him the recent bruises but I got the impression that he'd been down in the cellar several times before.

'When you get in that room with them, don't kick up a fuss,' he advised. 'They give you something to drink, makes everything easier. There's nothing you can do. Let's just hope they're in a good mood. They give us cigarettes as well then.'

He tried to give me an encouraging grin and shrugged his shoulders as if to say, 'What can you do?' then he tried to pull his costume down a little lower.

I noticed two of the boys were almost naked. They had tiny pieces of gold cloth tied around their waists that hardly covered their groins and more gold fabric made into collars was fastened around their necks.

The youngest boy, a stocky child aged no more than seven, was dressed as a cowboy. He looked sleepy, his face was flushed, his eyes drooped and he reminded me of Davie at that age. I wanted to take him from the room, take him somewhere safe, take us all somewhere safe, but there was nowhere to go.

'Come on, Robbie, there's nothing for it. Get the rest of that costume on,' Matt's voice broke into my thoughts.

'They'll be back in a minute and you don't want to be the one who makes them mad 'cos you're not ready.'

I wrapped the long dark cloak round me. It smelled of sweat. I could see that it was stained and just the feel of it made my bare skin crawl with disgust. When I pulled up the hood, a cold rubbery thing fell down and flapped against my face and I gave a startled little squeal.

'It's only a mask,' Matt said. 'Don't be scared of that.' He bent down, groped on the floor behind me and came up with a pair of old-fashioned, black, lace-up boots.

'I knew they would have left these for you,' he said. 'You have to put them on too.' Just looking at them I could tell that they were at least a couple of sizes too big and shook my head in disbelief.

'You must, they're part of your costume. They know I'll have told you to wear them, so we'll both be in trouble if you don't.'

I pulled them onto my bare feet. I was right – they were so loose that I could only shuffle in them.

The silvery-white garment that Christopher had been holding turned out to be a ballerina's dress. Its short skirt flared out over his tiny hips, his slender legs were bare and on his feet he wore dirty white satin ballet slippers. An imitation diamond necklace hung around his neck and sparkled in the candlelight, as did the tears that trickled down his smooth cheeks. He knew what was going to happen to him.

It always happened to him in the cellars.

I clutched the edges of the robe with one hand and looked down at the floor. Everything was blurred without my glasses so I picked them up instinctively and put them back on, but still I felt sick, dizzy and pathetic in the stupid costume. I waited for someone to laugh at me; not one boy did.

'Robbie, your glasses,' hissed Matt. 'Come on, quickly, take them off.'

I reluctantly placed them on top of my pile of clothes.

'Anyhow,' said Matt with a sad attempt at ironic bravado, 'you're better off not seeing those buggers, they're so bleeding ugly. And you certainly don't want to watch what goes on too closely.'

Just as he finished talking, the wardens were back. Blake caught hold of my head, inspecting my get-up. 'Good, Robbie,' he said, breathing more stale breath into my face. Parker had gone over to the boys in gold who were huddled in a corner, their hands trying to cover their lower bodies. He brought out two chain-link dog leads, clipped them onto the gold collars and held them in one black-gloved hand while in his other he carried a whip made out of a short piece of cane with thin pieces of cloth stuck to it. Although it was not designed to inflict much damage, it still clearly stung when he gave a test flick of it on the boys' bare skin.

'My pretty little slave boys,' he murmured as he jerked the leads to make them stand up. Blake pushed me forward and the 'slave boys' brought up the rear of our sad little column as we went through to the main room where another three men, including Anderson, were waiting.

'Hello, little boy,' said the man who visited us to the boy in the cowboy costume. 'Are you my own little coy boy?' His hand stretched out, caught hold of the boy's arm and gently pulled him closer. He pulled out a large black sweet and popped into the little boy's mouth. His cheek bulged as he sucked it, but unlike most children given a gobstopper his mouth did not turn up at the corners; neither did his eyes light up. He just stood passively by the man's side gazing blankly at him.

'Hey, Quasi,' called Parker. 'Be a good boy and fill my glass.'

He shoved it into my fist and pushed me towards a table where bottles of drink were standing. 'Make mine a whisky, old chap,' he said in mocking tones.

I stood there clutching my cloak round my naked body and feeling confused. Whilst I could recognise a gin bottle, which bottle had the whisky in it? And how much was I meant to pour into the glass?

Parker's booted foot swung out and caught me on my leg.

'Now, Quasi, now! I mean it! While you're there, fill two tumblers from the jug and bring them over here for my thirsty slave boys.' He giggled then, a sound that reminded me of Neville, and I shivered.

I shuffled over to the table, peered at the bottles and just managed to make out from the labels which one was whisky. All the time I was conscious of that hump, which rubbed against my skin, and my nudity under the cloak. I carried his drink over with one hand, and when I reached him his hand slid across my hooded head and back until it rested on the hump.

'Ugly sad little fucker, aren't you, Robbie?'

Again that giggle left his mouth. 'Bring both of their drinks at the same time. You've got two hands, so use them.'

I gave up the effort of clutching together the edges of my cloak. I somehow knew that if I stopped those futile efforts it would at least reduce some part of his sadistic enjoyment.

'Hey, Robbie,' said Blake in tones already blurred by alcohol, 'have a drag of this.' He passed me a rolled-up cigarette. I put it to my lips and dragged the smoke down into my lungs. It smelled and tasted funny, not at all like the Woodbines I had smoked before. He took it from me, sucked on it himself then passed it to Christopher, whose pale cheeks hollowed as he sucked as hard as he could. 'That's my girl, Chrissie! Take it deep!' Blake laughed at his own little joke, which no one else seemed to share.

'Have a drink as well, Robbie,' he said and filled a paper cup from the jug, then shoved it into my hands.

Suddenly I was aware of how parched my throat felt and I gulped it down. I poured out more drinks, dragged on another funny-smelling cigarette and drank some more of the lemonade-tasting drink.

Someone turned the light off, leaving the room lit only by the glow of the candles. Music came from a record player: something fast and rhythmic with drumbeats. My head spun, my myopic eyes darted around the room trying to see into the shadows. It was either after that second lemonade or the funny-smelling cigarette that everything seemed to have grown darker, the candlelight brighter, the men's faces larger, their laughter more raucous and every note of music sharper and clearer as it vibrated in my head.

The man who visited us patted my head. The little cowboy was sitting firmly on his knee, his thumb in his mouth and his eyes glazed. At some point his cowboy trousers had been removed.

Another man, who had not spoken since I had been in the room, told me to fetch him a drink. When I gave it to him his hand rubbed that hump before sliding under my cloak to fondle me. I felt his nails, long for a man's, digging into my skin, heard his breathing quicken, then his foot lashed out and I stumbled back. 'That's for being such an ugly little bastard,' he said and turned to Parker.

'Give me one of yours.' He stretched out his hand, caught hold of the boy's lead and pulled him over.

Other hands grabbed me and slid over my body, pinching and nipping at me. I know one of them was Anderson, the warden. The room spun.

My sight might have been very blurred but I could see the pretty boy being pulled down onto Blake's lap and I realised that the little boy in the cowboy outfit was not the only one whose trousers had been removed. I saw Blake's flushed face slobbering over Christopher's bejewelled neck and face while his hand moved up and down under the white ballerina skirt.

The man with the long nails took his boy into the shadows. I heard the noise of stinging slaps followed by a cry that was quickly muffled. A sigh of satisfaction followed, then loud groans and finally a shout. They didn't come out of the shadows for a long time.

I felt I was almost in a dream as the candles flickered. Whirls of smoke drifted into the air and the sweet smell of those cigarettes mixed with another smell I recognised – the one that reminded me of stale fish and sweat. Someone came over to me, placed another cigarette in my mouth and my eyes drooped. I felt hands on me, heard distant laughter.

'Watch the floor show,' a voice murmured in my ear, and through half-closed eyes I saw the two 'slave boys' placed head to groin and heard the swish of the silken whip as it rose and fell.

I tried to sit up but I couldn't; the room was spinning too much. My vision was blurring more and more. My gaze rested briefly on Matt. I saw his head bobbing up and down and his small hands resting on large hairy thighs.

More hands were touching me then, and I felt my hand being forced around a penis and moved up and down. Then someone was doing the same thing to me. Hands kneaded my backside and ran all over me. I mostly kept my eyes closed and just willed it to be over. Everything started to slow down, and at some stage I must have fallen asleep.

I awoke to feel someone shaking me.

'Party over,' said a voice and the two boys, Matt and I were taken to the room where our clothes were. A few minutes later we were back in our dormitory.

Christopher and the little 'cowboy' didn't appear until the next day. The little boy stared blankly at something only he could see and Christopher had dark circles under his eyes. As he turned his face away from us I saw glitter on his cheek.

'You OK?' Martin asked me gruffly after breakfast.

I nodded quickly. I didn't want to talk about it and I don't think he did either. But over the next few days, when we were on our own, I started asking Martin and Pete more about the parties. I needed to know, even though I could sense they didn't want to tell me.

'There's no point worrying,' Pete said. 'You're not one of the pretty ones so you probably won't be a regular. You might even get away with just your initiation party.' He shuddered, and I got the impression he was remembering his own. 'They lose interest when you get older. Once you're past twelve they don't bother so much.'

This was reassuring, but there was a part of me that needed to know the worst. I suppose I thought I could prepare myself in some way.

'It's the little ones I feel sorriest for, when they give it to them in the arse,' Martin said sadly. 'It never happened to me, thank God, but one boy told me that the pain goes right through your bottom and up to the top of your head. He said afterwards it hurt him to walk and that it bled out of his arse.'

I winced and screwed up my nose in sympathy. And then I had a horrible thought: was this what had happened to John?

'Have you heard about birthday parties?' Pete asked. 'Sometimes they have a birthday party for a boy. Take him in the middle of the night; sing happy birthday to him. Then one shoves his cock in the boy's mouth while another one squeezes his balls so hard it hurts. The boy can't scream or yell, because if he does and his teeth just touch that cock, there's another punishment waiting. They put him in a bath full of cold water, push his head under and hold him there until he chokes and starts to lose consciousness.'

We were all silent, thinking how terrifying this would be.

Martin spoke next, very quietly. 'A boy told me that the worst thing that ever happened to him was that they masturbated him until his cum squirted out. He said he felt like his own body had betrayed him, like they could control him completely. He really hated himself for that.'

I glanced at Martin and wondered if he was talking about something that had happened to him, but he wouldn't say any more.

'Just keep your head down,' Pete advised. 'As I said, you're lucky you haven't got your brother's looks.'

Now I knew more about what happened at parties, I became even more anxious when the men crept into our dormitory at night. Would it be my turn again? What would happen to me next time? And when the footsteps went past my bed and stopped by someone else's, the relief was overwhelming.

Chapter Thirty-three

When I look back on those days at Haut de la Garenne, of course much of it is blurred. I remember the staff lashing out at us for no reason. A hand would whack us across the head when we least expected it or a cane would land on the backs of our legs, but these were such daily occurrences that they ceased to be remarkable. I remember the terror of being taken down for a party and not knowing what the night would bring. Although I got off lightly, probably because I was plainer-looking and older than most of the boys there, I saw some horrific sights.

I do remember that there were snatches of normality, that there were times when we forgot to be scared, times when we played games, times we laughed, times we ran in the fresh air, times when we forged friendships and even snatched quiet, private time when I liked to curl up under a tree and read.

Some memories have receded and become part of the grey fabric of my early life while others are so powerful that they have overshadowed them.

Three of those memories have left their imprint firmly
in my mind – imprints that, as hard as I might try, will
never be erased.

The first was when one of us fell in love.

Our group were all at the age, somewhere between thirteen and fourteen and a half, when hormones start to waken,
and girls, who were once seen as playmates, someone to
laugh with and tease, have turned into mystifying strangers.

Pete was fourteen when that happened to him. Only a
few months younger than him, I was curious, even
vaguely interested, but not to the extent that it ruled my
life. So at the time I didn't see what all the fuss was about
when Pete fell in love.

Her name was Dianne. She was pretty – even I could
see that; a tiny, fine-boned, thirteen-year-old girl with long,
straight blonde hair that fell in a silky curtain to her shoulders. Her clear skin was like peaches and cream, her nose
small and her mouth full and pretty. Her huge blue eyes
looked at her surroundings and us with very little interest.

Pete's eyes had picked her out the moment she came
into the home. We all wondered why she had been put
there. She didn't look as though she was a habitual
shoplifter or disappeared for days and refused to say
where she had been or who with. But we did recognise the
aura that clung to her: a mixture of crumpled innocence,
hurt and vulnerability, which she tried hard to conceal.

Pete was besotted within hours of first seeing her and
made it his business to find out as much about her as he
could from the other girls.

Dianne's mother had remarried and within days of that ceremony had complained one moment that her daughter resented her new stepfather then the next that she had tried to seduce him. She said she could no longer cope with her teenage daughter and couldn't be expected to tolerate her behaviour in the marital home.

Dianne's story was rather different; according to her, the new stepfather had tried to paw her with his sweaty hands at every opportunity. At first she said nothing to her mother and just tried to avoid being alone with him. That worked until the day she returned home from school to find he had left work early and was waiting for her in the empty house.

She managed to fight him off and run to her mother's workplace. There, between heaving sobs, she told her what had happened.

The mother wanted her new husband more than she wanted Dianne. She went to the welfare office and the authorities chose to believe the adults' version of events, that Dianne had tried to seduce him. We, on the other hand, all believed Dianne.

Lots of boys tried to talk to her but her blue eyes just looked indifferently back before she ducked her head and hid behind that curtain of silky blonde hair. But somehow Pete, with his puppy-dog devotion, gained her interest.

It might have seemed a long time to him before she allowed her small hand to be held by his larger one, but it was only about a week. Even a day seems like forever to a lovesick teenager. When it happened he was ecstatic; a huge grin was plastered across his face, and at every chance he got he bored us with his constant references to his darling's perfections.

Martin, Marc and I would look at each other, raise supercilious eyebrows and smirk. But he was oblivious to our boyish mockery, for Pete was in the thralls of first love.

They met outside in the gardens and went to a place where they thought thick bushes would conceal them. Innocent kisses were exchanged, arms went around slim shoulders, a blonde head nestled trustingly against Pete's chest. In the common room and at meals their eyes met, they smiled small private smiles with each other, and laughed at jokes only they could understand.

I can't say that at the time I didn't feel a spark of jealousy creeping in. Pete was our mate; we all did things together. But the other side of me somehow felt warmed by it. It was a slice of happiness that I, on the outside, could still enjoy.

But of course it was only ever going to be a temporary happiness. Without knowing it, Pete had broken a basic rule of survival: don't show interest in someone a warden wants for himself.

Pete and Dianne were seen together and it was noted; being young and still retaining some naivety, they took fewer and fewer precautions. All of us knew about the pretty boys, and we had all experienced beatings, but somehow we never thought that anything much happened to the girls.

They waited, those wardens; bided their time. They didn't just want her; they wanted Pete to learn his lesson as well.

When she was fast asleep they came for her. There were three of them. She was no match for them, and even if she had been able to run, where could she have gone?

She was so light that all they had to do was pick her up out of her bed and carry her down to the cellars. They didn't touch Pete; there was no need to. They would enjoy watching him suffer later.

At first she refused to speak to him the next morning. 'Go away,' she said when he came up to her.

'What's wrong?' he asked when he saw the pallor of her face and the downcast eyes with lids that were swollen from her tears. She shrugged off his hand, turned her head from him and walked away.

He followed her. He had seen the bruises on her face: the ones just under her ears, the mark a hand makes when it holds down a head.

'Who did it to you?' he pleaded.

'No one did anything,' she said. 'Leave me alone.'

He walked away, head down, feet dragging, looking like a puppy whose owner had just kicked him.

He begged her to talk to him. For days she didn't.

During those days she walked with her arms wrapped around her body as though to hold her pain in. Every night they came and took her, until she no longer even tried to resist.

In the end she told Pete what those men had done. How they had held her down and pulled her nightdress up. Somehow, she said, that felt even worse than if they had removed it. Two of them held her legs and arms apart, the third raped her. She bled a little that first time.

'My first virgin,' he said with a satisfied smirk.

'They're the best,' said the second one, before ramming himself into her.

'It hurt,' she said. 'It hurt a lot.'

They gave her a drink, which made her drowsy, took some of the pain away. Then the third one had her; he told her he was going to outlast his two colleagues. She didn't know if he had or not because everything went fuzzy. They told her then that she was theirs; that they could have her whenever they wanted.

'I'll tell,' she said. 'I'll tell.'

They had laughed at her then. 'What? Your own mother said you were a dirty little whore, always after your stepdaddy, so who's going to believe you?'

That was the first night; the second and the third it was the same. She drank the drink they gave her and smoked those sweet cigarettes. On the fourth and fifth nights they tried something new. This time when they took her down to the cellars they gave her the drink first and put a cigarette in her hand, the type that made the world seem better. They caught hold of her, but more gently this time, then they entered her, all three of them, each one choosing a different orifice. They were careful not to be too rough, so she wasn't badly injured. They took it in turns moving her into different positions and in between she gulped the drink down and dragged more of the sweet-smelling smoke deep into her lungs. Finally, they cast her aside; a discarded broken plaything they no longer wanted.

So she told Pete. She wanted someone to tell her it wasn't her fault.

But Pete was too young, and besides, what could he do? He wasn't capable of mending her or even comforting her. I bumped into him just after he'd heard all this and he blurted it out to me in a state of shock.

'How could they?' he kept asking. 'How could they?'

I tried my best to get him to calm down to no avail.

'I can't bear it,' he said. 'I have to get out of here.'

'Don't, Pete. You know what will happen if you run away.'

But he wasn't listening. He was in such a state that he just started running and I watched him as he took off down the road and became a speck on the horizon.

It was several days later when we heard what happened to him. I guess one of the wardens told some of the boys and they came to tell Martin and me.

Pete had been picked up by the police and put in the back of their car. He must still have been burning up with rage at every beating, every torture and every act of sexual abuse that had been inflicted on him during his time in the home mingled with his grief and rage at Dianne's destruction. With a scream it all burst out of him. He reached over the seat, put his hands around the policeman's neck and squeezed. The police car swerved, Pete's arms were forced down and handcuffs came out.

He was not brought back to Haut de la Garenne. He was taken instead to the mental hospital where he was wrapped in a straitjacket.

Dianne was also transferred. I heard she went to the unmarried mothers' home.

Chapter Thirty-four

The next memory that's imprinted on my brain is the one that haunts me the most. The morning I had my first inkling of it was about a year before I left the home.

We knew something had happened, something that wasn't good. The head warden looked stern, the other wardens were quiet and some of the boys were pale-faced and visibly shaken.

'What's happened?' I asked Marc that morning. The boys who were upset were from his dormitory. He turned to me and his face looked almost haggard. He told me that a boy, someone I had seen around but not known, had run away. Well, he had left the grounds.

'There's nothing new in that,' I said, puzzled by the serious look on Marc's face and the tense atmosphere.

'No, Robbie, it's not just that. He hung himself.'

'Poor sod,' I said sadly. 'But why did he do it? He'd got out, hadn't he?'

'Don't be stupid,' said Marc almost impatiently. 'He knew he would get caught. And he knew what they would do to him.'

I knew too. In the short time I had been in Haut de la Garenne there had been several attempts to escape, most recently Pete's. Each time I heard of boys running away I wondered where they thought they could run to. Jersey was an island, and no one would sell one of us a ferry ticket to leave it. All they achieved out there was a few hours of dreamed-of freedom before the police found them and brought them back. My mind went to the time in the orphanage when Marc and I had thought it was worth it, and the outcome of that escapade.

I wondered if those boys who tried to run away didn't remember seeing other white-faced culprits being dragged to the cellars for punishment the moment the police car drove away. Sometimes they were in there for a couple of days and sometimes longer. But regardless of the length of time spent down there, they were always quiet and subdued when they were finally released.

Sometimes they became the same as the boys who were taken regularly to the cellars for punishment: withdrawn and antisocial. It wasn't that they seemed content with their own company, but that they seemed unable to cope with anyone else's for long. Some would wander aimlessly in the grounds, and there were a few who, like Marc, had become angry and hurt after their beating.

Marc remained aloof from the other boys in the home, except for me. It was as though his anger set him apart. His voice broke into my thoughts: 'He would have been out in a year too,' he said sadly.

'Guess that just seemed too long a time,' I answered.

'Guess it did,' he replied, and sighed deeply.

We didn't say much after that, but all that day and for several days after I thought about that boy I hadn't known. I thought of his misery, a misery that must have been a reflection of my own, and for the first time in a year I felt hot tears flood my eyes.

What was going to happen to us? I asked myself. Where would we fit in once we left Haut de la Garenne on our fifteenth birthdays? I clenched my fists until my fingernails made deep, painful marks on my palms, and forced myself to think of John. John was my future. I knew he was waiting for me to come out of the home and then we would wait together for Davie to come out of the orphanage. When those days finally came we would be a family again: us three against the world.

It was that dream, which I knew one day would become a reality, that made those days bearable. But I was old enough then to wonder what happened to the boys who had no one. What did they do?

Twice now I had been given an answer to that question. First by Jimmy and then by the boy I didn't know. I cried then. For them. For all of us.

The shock over the death of the boy I didn't know gradually subsided. No one else had tried to run away but Marc seemed more distant than ever. He was a few months older than me and would be allowed to leave the home before I was, but given his recent remoteness I had already begun to miss our friendship that had endured for so many years. I guessed that Martin would be quite pleased when he left, because Marc's aloofness kept him outside our little circle, no matter how hard I tried to draw him in.

'Marc,' I said one morning when it was just the two of us. We were sitting in a corner of the grounds where we felt we were unobserved. 'You'll be out before me. What are you going to do?'

A frightened expression momentarily settled on his face, replacing the tough mask that he normally wore.

'I dunno,' he replied. 'There's no one waiting for me outside. Who's going to want to know us there? We're different, you know.'

I wanted to say that we were almost a family. Hadn't we been friends since we were little? I chose my words carefully as I tried to convey how I felt.

'But Nicolas will be leaving Sacre Coeur soon and I've only got a year to go before I'm fifteen. We can all meet up again. Maybe share a house or something. You could live at the hostel with John until I get out.'

Marc gave me a look that made words unnecessary, that told me I just didn't understand.

'John's your brother and so's Davie,' he said finally. 'You're all family.' He spoke as though that word excluded the rest of the world from being with us.

I searched for words to tell him that I thought of him as family but I couldn't find them.

That was the last conversation I ever had with Marc.

He wasn't at supper that evening, and by bedtime boys were whispering to each other, speculating about where he might have gone. It was two days later when the news of his fate reached Haut de la Garenne and spread almost instantly around wardens and boys alike. When I heard, it was like being punched hard in the stomach. I couldn't breathe for the pain.

Marc had made it clear by his actions that he didn't want to be cut down from a tree. He didn't want to be found with his tongue poking out between his blue-tinged lips. Neither did he want anyone's last memory of him to be of the piss and shit that had stained his legs. Nor did he want to be placed in a coffin; he was scared of the dark.

He went into town without permission, not that that really mattered. He went straight to a camping shop and bought canisters of butane gas, the sort people use for camping stoves.

He took them down into a wartime bunker half a mile from the home, a place where we had slipped off from time to time to have a sneaky smoke.

He used a pocket knife to pierce the canisters and lit a match.

I hope it was quick for him after he ignited that gas.

He had his wish; his body was not placed in a coffin and lowered into the ground. There was very little left to bury.

Chapter Thirty-five

Marc's death was just before my fourteenth birthday but when it came I was in no mood for celebrating. The only thing that cheered me up slightly was when Blake told me that I would now be allowed to leave the home once a month to go into town, so long as I asked for permission first.

The very next Saturday I headed into St Martin to look for John. I'd heard from other boys that he would probably be staying in one of the hostels for Haut de la Garenne leavers, and I asked at all of them until someone said yes, he had a room there. I sat on the steps and waited, and an hour or so later John came round the corner with a couple of friends, looking very grown-up in smart trousers and a shiny blue jacket.

'Robbie!' he yelled, and came running up and slapped me on the back.

We went to a café nearby and just talked for ages. I told him all about Marc dying and he frowned and shook his head sadly and sighed. 'Of course he could have lived with us. Stupid idiot!' He patted my shoulder sympathetically.

He asked how I was doing with my schoolwork and what I was planning to do when I left.

'I wanted to be a draughtsman, maybe do some kind of engineering drawing,' I told him, 'but the teacher says I would have to stay on at school longer. So I've decided to leave at fifteen and they've got me an apprenticeship with an electrician.' I looked at him anxiously, seeking his approval.

'Good,' he nodded. 'Get away from school as soon as you can.'

It was so wonderful being with him again that I nearly lost track of time, but John was keeping an eye on the clock. 'Don't be late back or they won't let you come again,' he said. We arranged where we would meet the following month, then he walked me part of the way back to Haut de la Garenne.

The third memory that's imprinted on my brain is a mixture of pain and triumph – but it was the pain that came first.

A couple of weeks after my visit to John, I heard that Davie was being transferred to Haut de la Garenne. He had been too disruptive. The nuns had tried solitary confinement and probably several other punishments but to no avail.

Spud and his bullying friends came up to me that morning.

'Oy, Garner,' said Spud. 'Heard your baby brother's arriving soon. Prettier than you, is he?'

At that moment Parker appeared and I knew from his face who had told Spud.

'Go on, answer them, Robbie. Don't be rude,' he ordered.

A wide smirk spread across Spud's face. 'Hey, Parker, do you think the baby one's as pretty as John?'

I thought of Davie's trusting face and his complete inability to suss people out.

'Oh God,' I thought. 'All these bastards have to do is tell him there's a bag of sweets for him if he goes with them.'

Reading my mind, they laughed.

'Hear he might be a bit friendlier than that big brother of yours. He's a miserable bugger is your John. Heard the little one might like fancy dress and parties.'

They all sniggered at that, especially Parker.

I didn't react so they soon got bored with their game.

Parker sneered at me, 'Go on, Garner, get lost. You're not worth bothering with.'

I didn't need any persuasion to move away as quickly as I could.

That group had always scared me, and when I heard about Davie's imminent arrival I panicked. Even though it was the middle of the day and there was a good chance I'd be missed, I left the grounds and ran into town to find John. Breathless, I blurted out the story about Davie's fall in the orphanage and how trusting and innocent he had become now. I told him about the transfer and the thinly veiled threats from Parker and the bullies. I asked him if we could all run away together to save Davie from what surely lay in wait for him.

John put his hand on my shoulder and said, 'Calm down,' but I could tell he was worried. He thought for a bit. 'Running away's not the answer. Don't think I haven't thought about it. But you're too young to get a job, you haven't got any references and you'll end up back there or on the streets. You're doing all right with your schooling. Don't want to mess that up. You've even got an apprenticeship lined up. No, you have to stay put.'

'But what about Davie?' I asked in despair.

'I want you to stop worrying. If you can keep your head down for a few days then you'll be all right. Those evil buggers won't hurt you or touch Davie. Trust me,' he said, and somehow I did.

Of course they caught me returning. They guessed where I had been. In bed that night, I was dreaming of running along the beach but suddenly my legs wouldn't move. I tried to put one in front of the other but nothing happened. There was something heavy pressing down on me, keeping me there. I heard a voice whispering to me. My eyes sprang open. It was Blake. His hands were pressing on my chest, holding me firmly against the mattress.

'Garner, you've been bad,' he said. I smelled the fumes on his breath and knew he had been drinking. Another figure emerged behind him. I saw Parker and my heart sank. Parker liked hurting people. I tried to open my mouth to tell them that I didn't know what they were talking about, but already hands were under the bedclothes, pulling at my arms, rolling me out of that warm sanctuary.

I felt a knee in my back, a hand in my hair. My arm was behind my back and, as I had seen happen to other boys, I was propelled from the room.

A hand covered my mouth, but even if I had been able to scream, it would have been useless. Everyone in the dormitory would have tried to still their breathing, tried not to draw attention to themselves. I wondered how many boys were peeping through their eyelashes at me and wondered if they felt grateful that it was me who was being taken and not one of them. Of course they did.

They dragged me down the dimly lit corridor to the stairs that led to the cellars. They were pushing me so hard that I slipped and nearly fell down those narrow steps.

They took me to a room that I hadn't been in before; a room that was almost square, without any furniture, but with a bath that resembled a large trough in the centre.

'Take your clothes off, Garner.'

I began to shake. Parker smirked, moved towards me, pulled the cord of my pyjamas with one hand and yanked them down with the other.

'You've been out with that brother of yours. We saw you. Thought you were clever, didn't you? We told you, Garner, you have to get permission. That cocky bastard brother of yours should have known that too.'

I opened my mouth to deny it as a vicious punch in the stomach made me double up, gasping for air.

'We didn't say you could talk,' shouted Blake and I heard Parker snigger again.

He let me watch what he did next. His eyes gleamed when he saw the fear that must have been written all over my face. He picked up a towel, slowly wrapped it round a piece of metal piping and slammed it into my ribs. The air rushed out of my lungs and through my mouth. I spun round and Blake's belt slammed hard against my legs. I was naked from the waist down and clutched my hands in front of me to try to protect myself.

Behind me I heard water gushing into the bath. Twice more that pipe whipped across my ribs. I fell down and my pyjama jacket was pulled off me. Two pairs of hands lifted me up and threw me into the icy water.

I felt the warmth of a body just behind my head and again the whiff of alcohol reached my nostrils.

'I think we should drown you, Garner. You're such a useless little sneak.'

It was Parker's voice, and his hand that went round my neck. My eyes goggled with fear, my legs thrashed, my arms flayed uselessly in the air. I tried to pull at that hand, but the grip only tightened. My head went under the water. I tried to hold my breath but couldn't. Water went up my nose, into my mouth and everything started going black.

They pulled me out of the bath, laid me on the floor and thumped my back until I vomited up the water I had swallowed, laughing all the while, then they left me wet and shivering in that chilly room.

I curled up on the floor shaking not only with cold but also with fright. I knew the door had been locked from the outside because I'd heard them do it as they left.

I don't remember how long I lay there. I fell into a dazed sleep and was woken by a foot kicking me in the ribs. Again I felt the flick of Blake's belt against my naked flesh and curled up even tighter to try and protect myself. A hand grabbed my hair, yanked it hard, and pain tore through my scalp. I crawled up onto my knees, trying to lessen the pain in my head.

'Get up, Garner,' ordered Blake. I stood shakily, hanging my head.

'We're going to take you back now, Garner. So what do you do the next time you want to see your brother?'

'Ask permission,' I replied softly.

He threw my pyjamas at me and told me to put them on. My fingers were so numb from cold that I couldn't do up the buttons on my jacket.

They laughed at me.

'Not such a cocky one now, is he?' Parker asked Blake.

'Nah, he's a pathetic little creep this one.'

'What are you, Garner? Say it, go on say it.' Parker was in front of me, his cold eyes looking into mine.

'I'm a pathetic little creep,' I repeated, trying not to cry.

They took me back to the dormitory and I climbed into my bed. I wanted to crawl under the bedclothes and stay there forever. I wanted to feel safe, but I had forgotten what that feeling was like.

Chapter Thirty-six

I can't remember if the sun was high in the sky or if grey clouds threatened rain the Sunday morning when I heard about Parker. I do remember exactly where I was, but not what I was doing.

I'd finished breakfast, gone outside and wandered to a corner of the grounds where Marc and I used to sit talking. Since Marc's death, I'd started avoiding the company of other boys, feeling the need to be alone more and more often. I wanted my old friend back. It wasn't something as simple as loneliness that I felt but an emptiness that not even my occasional meetings with John filled. The other boys had started to get irritated by my sudden aloofness but that just made me want to keep my distance even more. They had never been close to Marc and they had no experience of what it was like when a close friend killed himself. No matter how much you tell yourself it wasn't your fault, the dark side of your brain keeps prodding your conscience and saying if you had been a better friend he might have had the strength to cope.

What made everything more difficult was that we knew not to talk about the suicides anywhere near the wardens. When we were out of earshot, we asked each other how long the wardens thought they could keep everything quiet. Surely now there would be questions asked about why boys were so depressed that they killed themselves? At any rate, I hoped there would be. 'They' might not believe us if we told stories, but surely dead boys wouldn't go unnoticed?

When I shared these thoughts with John he gave me a look that was both impatient and pitying.

'You don't get it, do you, Robbie?' he said. 'There's no one who cares what happens to us. Why do you think we were put in the home in the first place? Because we were a problem to someone, a problem that no one wanted. No, it won't be the authorities that do anything.' I hadn't taken very much notice of his last comment but I remembered it later.

That morning, when I saw Martin running towards me I just wondered what he wanted. I could tell he was excited, but I wasn't particularly interested in finding out what it was about.

'Hey, Robbie, have you heard?' he asked.

'Heard what?'

'They say it was your brother, but no one knows for sure.'

My heart jumped. Had something happened to John? He saw the look on my face and hastened to reassure me.

'Nah, he's all right, nothing's happened to him.' A huge wolfish grin spread across his face. 'It's happened to that bastard Parker, though!'

I thought of Parker and how he had taunted me about Davie, those cruel cold eyes that slid over my body and his high-pitched sniggers when he hurt someone.

'He got beat up real bad,' Martin continued with a note of unmistakable glee in his voice. 'He's in the hospital.'

Maybe I should have found it in me to express some sympathy, some concern for his well-being, but all I felt was a sharp lifting of my spirits.

'He was found in the gents' lavatories. Whoever did it, and they reckon it must have been more than one attacker, broke his arm, his right one, really badly. They say you could see the bones sticking out like someone stamped on it hard. He's got a few cracked ribs as well.'

'Anything else?' I asked.

'He was unconscious when he was found, must have been the pain. Had to be taken off in an ambulance. The police were at the hospital.'

I felt a slight sense of unease then.

'Did he say who did it?' I asked.

'No.' Martin nearly doubled up with laughter. 'The idiot said he never saw them, that the men who did it attacked him from behind. But he was lying by the wash-basins when they found him. And what do washbasins have over them?'

'Mirrors!' I said. I grinned at the thought of Parker combing back his hair, then seeing someone behind him he really didn't want to see.

'Of course he knows who it was, but he's too scared to talk. And I'll tell you this and all: those wardens are looking worried. John's teamed up with a couple of other boys from here and Sacre Coeur; your pal Nicolas is one of them.'

'But they don't know each other!' I exclaimed, feeling puzzled.

'But they both know you, Robbie. They both know Davie. They're just warning those bleeding sods to lay off you both. Telling them that if you get hurt again they will find out who did it. Don't you see?' He paused. 'I hope some more of those bastards get hurt!' I knew that he must miss Pete as much as I was missing Marc, but at least his friend was still alive, albeit incarcerated in a mental hospital.

Davie arrived soon after that. It was almost three years since we last saw each other but he hadn't changed much. He was taller, of course, but he was still emotionally subdued and slow to respond when you asked him anything. He told me Sister Claire had left and he sounded as though he was sadder about that than he had been when I left. His trusting little face looked up at me.

'Is it nice in here?' he asked.

'It's not too bad,' I told him, crossing my fingers.

After Parker's 'accident' the wardens left me alone, as did the bullies, but I would always remember who they were and what they had done. At least during those last months at Haut de la Garenne, while I studied as hard as I could, I knew that Davie would be all right.

I knew that the bullies were aware that when I left there would be another one of us Garners on the outside;

another one who knew where they went for a drink, what they did on their days off. That, I prayed, would be enough to keep Davie safe.

Chapter Thirty-seven

Before the sun had tinged the sky pink, before the birds awoke to sing their chorus welcoming the new day, and before there were any sounds in the dormitory apart from the deep breathing of sleeping boys, I woke.

It was the early hours of my fifteenth birthday. For the last nine years my birthday hadn't been celebrated, but this was going to be different, I told myself. This was the day I had waited for with impatience, with apprehension and most of all with hope. It was the day that I was finally going to leave Haut de la Garenne.

Mr Smith, the welfare officer who three years earlier had told me how much I would enjoy Haut de la Garenne, was coming to collect me after breakfast. He was taking me to what he referred to as a hostel, one of a number of large terraced houses that had been converted specifically to cater for teenagers like us.

I had been given a pair of grey trousers and a jacket to wear when I left. As I lay in bed I pictured the day that lay in front of me; the day that John had promised would come, the day that we would finally be together again. I knew there were hours to go, formalities to be completed and paperwork to be filled in, but nothing, simply nothing was going to stop me going through those doors and joining the outside world.

I had packed my few possessions the night before. There wasn't much: an old pair of jeans, a shirt, a jumper and a change of underwear. A few toiletry articles, a pen, my drawing pencils and my sketchpads were the sum total of my meagre worldly possessions. But I didn't mind. I had my apprenticeship as an electrician to start the following Monday, a small income of my own to look forward to and a new life in front of me, one I would be sharing with my older brother.

As soon as the other boys stirred, I dressed in my new clothes and went to the dining room to join Davie for my last breakfast at Haut de la Garenne. I was sad about leaving him yet again but he'd be leaving himself in two years. We had learnt to accept that a year wasn't such a long time and two years was just twice not such a long time. Anyhow, that's what we'd said to each other the night before. I had wanted to say my real goodbyes then, so as not to cloud my special day.

No sooner had I swallowed my last mouthful than one of the members of staff requested that I make my way to the head warden's office.

Apart from my first day there, it was the only time I had entered that office without fear. There was nothing he could do to me now, I told myself. I knocked and when he called 'Enter!' I pushed the door open and came face to face with a man who seemed smaller and more insignificant than he had ever done before. He wore his formal mask, the one he showed to welfare officers and the police, the mask of good-natured concern. It was almost impossible to detect the power-mad sadist who controlled this regime of terror and corruption, where some members of staff took pleasure in terrorising vulnerable children.

He shook my hand as though he had my best interests at heart and I, against my will, was sucked into his act and played out my role. Politely and without emotion I thanked him for my time there.

Next I went back to my dormitory and said goodbye to my few friends. The usual promises were made about keeping in touch and meeting up again when they were released. Few would be kept, though, because we all wanted to put our time there behind us.

After that I just sat on my bed and waited for Mr Smith to arrive. Davie sat quietly next to me. His bottom lip trembled as he said what he had said three years earlier.

'I know you have to go, Robbie. But it won't be for ever, will it?'

'No, Davie,' I said, 'it won't be for ever. And when you come out John and I will both be waiting for you. We will all have a home together again.'

His trusting face smiled at me. 'Will I have a room of my own?'

'Yes, Davie,' I replied, and he looked pleased.

I peered out of the dormitory window. 'What time does Mr Smith eat his breakfast? Where is he?' I wondered impatiently. And suddenly he was there.

'Well, Robbie lad,' he said by way of greeting. 'Ready to start your new life?'

Words simply failed me. Instead I felt my face stretch into a wide grin. I hugged Davie quickly, then I picked up my bag and followed Mr Smith down the stairs, out of the doors, to the car park, into his car, out through the gates, and at last I was free.

Mr Smith was driving a bright turquoise Ford Anglia. As soon as it pulled up at our destination, John was there. He opened the door, I jumped out and for a moment we forgot that we were meant to be grown-ups and hugged each other tightly. Tears streamed down my cheeks but for the first time since I was five they were tears of utter joy.

There was a flurry of activity as Mr Smith introduced me to the owners of the hostel, then he was gone and John and I were left grinning like idiots at each other.

I had been put in the same dormitory as him, a room with only five beds. I already knew two of the boys in our room, although not well. They had come out of the home a few months before me. John told me that they and the third boy, who had been there for over a year, didn't socialise very much.

'We've tried to get them to come out with us but they won't. That bleeding place, it's done something to them. I've said to them not to let it beat them. "Don't let those bastards win," I've told them, but they don't listen. They have terrible nightmares.' He paused briefly and looked away. 'We all do. We can't help what happens in our sleep, can we? Anyhow all they say is that they want to save up their money and get off this bleeding island. They never want to see anyone from there again. Can't say I blame them. They don't talk much, just watch television in the evenings and drink beer together. Anyhow, enough about them! It's your birthday and I've got to get you some new gear. Can't have my baby brother looking square, can I?'

He beamed at me. 'We're going shopping. And then you are going to have your first pint of beer. It doesn't matter that you're not eighteen yet; don't worry about the pub because a mate of mine works there. Anyhow, when I've got you looking sharp, no one will know you're only fifteen.' As John had only just turned eighteen himself, I guessed he knew his way around all the important minor things of life like underage drinking.

'Nicolas's meeting up with us in the pub,' he added.

'Where's he living?' I asked, excited at the prospect of seeing my old childhood friend.

'Another hostel just spitting distance from here. But he'll come back here later, and after we've all had supper and changed we're going out to celebrate your birthday and your freedom from that place!'

We walked to the main street; John already knew which shops to take me to. At the first one he bought me a tight-fitting pair of Levi jeans. They were the new, straight-legged ones, so tight that I wondered how I was going to sit down. Next stop was for shoes. My first pair of grown-up ones were bright blue with long pointed toes.

'Winkle pickers', John called them and assured me they were the height of fashion.

Then it was the pub, the Eagle Tavern. It was here where, on my fifteenth birthday, I was introduced to my first pint of beer.

There was an old jukebox in the corner. I had never seen one before and John had to show me how it worked, giving me the right change. I put on 'Good Luck Charm', one of Elvis Presley's latest releases.

Nicolas turned up clutching a birthday card in his hand. He was a taller and older-looking Nicolas with very little left of the freckle-nosed boy who had once looked at life with such a hopeful smile. He ruffled my hair and I threw my arms around him and squeezed him tight. Being tactile was not something I found easy – even now I like to keep my physical distance from other people – but he was my childhood friend and I was just so happy to see him.

He was coming up to eighteen but looked older than his years. I think we all did. We stepped apart and punched each other on the arm as we hid our embarrassment at our display of emotion.

'We'd better celebrate, Robbie,' he said, ignoring the fact that I already had a pint glass in front of me. He sauntered to the bar and came back with what he called a 'brown boiler', which I discovered was half brown ale and half mild.

'Don't get him any more!' John warned him, and then gave me a cheeky smile to take the edge off his remark.

'Can't get drunk yet, Robbie. We've got a long day all planned for you. You need to pace yourself.'

I sat there just soaking up the atmosphere in that smoky, beer-smelling pub. Nicolas and John talked about going to the dance hall and ribbed me about getting a girl-friend. After we finished our drinks, we wandered back to the hostel in high spirits, eager to have our supper. Nicolas had left his change of clothes there earlier and John, ever persuasive, had arranged with the owners to let him have his dinner with us.

My birthday dinner was a mixed grill and several thick slices of bread and butter, all washed down with numerous cups of strong tea. Although the one thing that had been good at Haut de la Garenne was the food, somehow the first meal I ate in freedom tasted just wonderful.

When I had finished I nearly left the table to go and ask the couple in charge of the hostel for permission to go out. I half rose from the table, then stopped.

'Where do you think you're off to?' John asked.

I told him what had gone through my head.

'Yes,' he said, 'I was like that for a long time. But, little brother, you're free now and don't you forget it.'

After supper we showered and I changed into my new clothes. I slid into my tight jeans, buttoned up my shirt then put on a black jacket with shiny lapels that John had lent me. John and Nicolas dressed in smart rocker suits: silver grey for Nicolas, bright blue for John. String ties were knotted, pointed-toe shoes pulled on and Brylcreem was applied, giving John and Nicolas fashionable quiffs and me a sort of sleeked-back look.

'It'll grow,' John said kindly, looking at my short hair. Out we went again.

I felt very sophisticated when we drank French red wine at a bar instead of beer.

'Right,' said Nicolas when a whole bottle had been consumed, 'we're going to a dance and you are going to meet a girl!' He led the way to Springfield's, the local dance hall.

Once inside we chose a table near the dance floor. It made me feel part of the crowd. I enjoyed watching my brother and my old friend saunter up to pretty girls. I enjoyed seeing them take an outstretched hand, lead the girl onto the floor and, fascinated, I watched their feet fly and their hips swing as they jived to the rock-and-roll music that was booming out.

'Next time we'll teach you how to pick up girls,' they both said, laughing. 'And I'll teach you to jive too, Robbie,' John added.

Suddenly I felt an intense happiness that brought a surge of blood rushing to my face. It was the thrill of simply being young combined with the dawning realisation that life might just turn out to be an adventure. Nicolas and John thought I was blushing and laughed even louder. I didn't feel a need to correct them.

Later that night there was only John and me left. Nicolas had disappeared with a girl.

We strolled down to the beach. The air was still warm from the afternoon sun. A slight breeze blew small clouds of sand off crumbling sandcastles and touched my face with a light caress. Marc came into my mind then – Marc as he had been on that night we had spent on the beach. I felt a twinge of sadness and pushed it aside. Marc would want me to be happy, I thought. He had been adamant that I would be reunited with John and he would be pleased that I finally was.

Suddenly John asked me, in a hesitant voice: 'Robbie, I know about the beatings, but did anyone, you know, touch you when you were in those places? When you were small, did the bigger boys do anything to you?'

I pictured the nuns washing my tiny penis when I was still only five and a half, pulling and jerking it as they washed it. It was as though that piece of flesh was separate from my body and they wanted to hurt it; after those bath times it had smarted when I peed.

I thought of Neville and the way he had hung Davie and me up next to the freshly killed chickens. And while those headless birds spurted blood and flapped their wings he put his hands inside our trousers. And I remembered what he had done then.

And I felt that terror of being small and at an adult's mercy. I remembered how we had been mocked, bullied and degraded by them.

Finally I thought of the cellars, the parties, what I had seen there and what I had felt.

'No,' I said, 'it happened to some of my friends, but not to me.'

I heard John breathe a huge sigh of relief. He didn't look at me. We just kept walking along the sand as the air darkened around us and waves rolled up gently on the shore.

'And you?' I asked, pretending I'd never heard about John's experiences. I wondered what I would say if he told me the truth and at the same time I prayed that he wouldn't. 'In the home did the bigger boys touch you when you were small? Or those bastard wardens, did they do anything when you were in there?'

There was a silence and for a moment I thought he wasn't going to answer me. I didn't dare look at him.

'At night,' my brother said, 'after they'd been drinking, the wardens would come into our dormitories. They'd choose a boy, pull him out of bed and frog march him down to the cellars where they were partying.' He told me they were just little boys and they were shaking with fear because they'd heard what happened to children who were taken in the night. 'And down in the cellar, their faces were forced into pillows so they couldn't scream and those men hurt them. They hurt them badly.'

As he talked, John's pain rolled off him in waves. I wanted to say something, anything that would dispel it. But I remained silent. I wanted to reach out my hand to him, touch him, and comfort him as I had done when I was very young and he had wet the bed. But we weren't little boys any longer, so I didn't.

We reached a wall that ran along by the beach. He sat down on it and I sat beside him, then he took out his cigarettes, lit two and handed me one. He coughed as he inhaled deeply, blew out a puff of smoke and then carried on talking.

'There was a room in the basement where they locked boys away for days sometimes. And at night they raped them till they bled, or forced penises into mouths that were almost too small to take them. They had flabby, hairy stomachs and they smelled of sweat and cum.'

Tears were on my brother's face. Angry, hurt tears. I still remained silent.

'When those filthy old men came in their mouths, the boys would try hard not to swallow. But the men would see and they'd hold their noses, pinching so it hurt, until they just had to swallow because they had to breathe.'

'That's what happened to some of the boys there,' he said and I heard those words echo between us, words he found impossible to utter. 'But it didn't happen to me.'

He drew once more on his cigarette, then threw it on the ground. Slowly he squashed it flat with the sole of his shoe and stood up. We avoided each other's eyes. There were no more words that needed to be spoken between us for without them we had told each other everything.

We turned then. Our hands slid into our pockets, we stuck out our elbows, bent our heads and walked back to the hostel with big boys' bravado, whistling as we went.

Epilogue

There were questions about our past that both John and I wanted answered. First, I went to visit Stanley. I knew where he was – he'd never left the mental hospital. I pushed aside my childhood fear of the place and went to see him.

He had turned into an old man, one who seemed happy enough. We smoked a cigarette together and chatted about my work and what John and Davie were doing.

I didn't ask him why he had tried to hang himself or why he had left us. I wanted to, but I couldn't. Nor did he tell me.

Soon after this John told me he wanted to go to England. He had traced Gloria and wanted to confront her to get some answers. I said I would go with him; I wanted to put my past behind me and start a new life.

Before we left, we reminded the people who mattered at Haut de la Garenne that our friends would be keeping an eye on Davie. We warned them that England was only a short boat journey away.

As the ferry pulled out of St Helier, I felt I was leaving a chunk of my past behind me.

We'd heard that Gloria was staying in a small town in Suffolk. We got a train there and walked from the station to the address we'd been given – a nice semi-detached house on a quiet street.

Of course there was a man in her life, a small man of indeterminate age who provided her with gin and cigarettes.

'We're looking for our mother,' we said when he opened the door.

With a shell-shocked expression, he pushed the door till it was only open a crack and called out to Gloria.

'My sons!' she exclaimed, throwing the door wide with no sign of remorse or regret.

It was very strange seeing our mother again – not that we had ever called her that. No longer was she the voluptuous, red-haired Gloria of our memories but a middle-aged woman who had run to fat, with the soft stomach and wrinkled eyelids of the hardened drinker.

I can't remember the excuses she gave for leaving us, maybe because I didn't listen to them. I was only there for John's sake; as a little boy John had loved her, whereas I had loved him.

She enquired about our health and the size of our pay packets.

We told her about Davie's accident and the brain damage he had suffered but she showed no interest.

We asked what had happened to our sister.

'I came and took her,' she said.

She had gone to Sacre Coeur for Denise. It was just us she had left.

John went white. Shock robbed him of speech. I felt nothing. She showed no shame. As far as she was concerned, she'd done nothing wrong.

'Where is Denise?' John asked at last.

'She's staying at a friend's.'

I saw John clenching his fists but he didn't say anything. We caught eyes and it was me who spoke. 'We'd better be going now,' I said.

John had the answer he'd been looking for. It was lack of love that had made her leave us; that and the desire to be free.

He and I stayed in England and found work. I carried on training as an electrician; he went into sales.

We wrote brightly coloured postcards to Davie.

When he was ready to leave Haut de la Garenne, he was sent to work on a farm on Jersey. He needed an adult to care for him, they said.

When John was twenty-one he became Davie's legal guardian. We brought him to England and found him a job in a hotel as a kitchen porter. Finally he was given his own room.

I went to find my sister Denise. She looked like Gloria had once looked, but with a beehive hairstyle. We had nothing in common. The paths our lives had taken were too different. I didn't see her again.

Over the years, I found out what had happened to some of the other people I had known at Sacre Coeur and Haut de la Garenne.

When he was discharged from hospital, Pete disappeared into the flotsam of drifters who, having no roots or family, made alcohol their friend. He created a social circle by drinking with strangers in back-street bars, sometimes for an hour and sometimes for a whole day, until his anger came back and made him fight them.

Nicolas went to England and trained as a baker. He married and had a son. I know he gave him a puppy for his fifth birthday because we got a Christmas card that year with a photo of them all.

Christopher became a teenage prostitute who dressed in shiny girl's clothes. I heard he died of AIDS.

The pretty boys left the island. We never heard what happened to them.

We lost touch with Martin but I heard from someone that he got married three times.

Stanley died at the age of eighty.

Gloria died in her sixties. I didn't go to the funeral.

John didn't go to her funeral either because he died before her, of motor neurone disease. That terrible wasting illness put my brother in a wheelchair and eventually in a nursing home.

That was all a long time ago.

I have no photographs of us when we were young. There are no family snapshots of our growing years. But inside my head I keep an album and when I close my eyes I can open it and look at the pictures inside at my leisure and remember how we were.

John as he was at eight, a golden boy, running on the beach with a wide grin on his face and a stolen apple in his hand.

Davie at three, all curves and dimples, his arms waving in time to his ceaseless chatter.

John sitting on that wall at Sacre Coeur nearly seven years later, already looking like a man, his eyes sparkling as he said my name.

Davie at five, pale-skinned and thin, his mouth rarely smiling.

Him at ten and again at thirteen, his solemn face turned to me, his gaze holding mine as he asked that question: 'It won't be for ever, will it, Robbie?'

John at seventeen, so handsome, so confident that his past was left behind and his future stretched in front of him.

John in a wheelchair, his body drooping and his face lined.

John smiling up at me when I tucked his blanket round his knees, that smile that said, 'It's just you and me, brother, just you and me against the world.'

After I had buried my beautiful brother I did something I had wanted to do since I was a child and used to look out to sea.

I bought an air ticket.

'Do you want to come?' I asked Davie. 'Come with me to faraway places where the sun is hot and the sky is blue.'

'You go,' he said. 'I like my job. I like my room. It won't be for ever, will it, Robbie?'

'No, Davie. It won't be for long,' I promised him for the third time.

When my grief over John's death had lessened, I returned to England. Davie was still working in the hotel where he had the room of his own.

I got a room just near him and took a job as an engineer. I live on my own but I see Davie two or three times a week. We have dinner or go to the pub. He seems content with his life.

I thought my past was behind me – and then I turned on the television. 'Human remains have been found in the cellars underneath a children's home in Jersey,' the newscaster said.

For the rest of the week I tried to avoid the news. I stayed in, switched the television off, even refused to listen to the radio. But I found it impossible. Newspapers seemed to be everywhere: at the garage, the grocery store, even in the hands of my fellow workers, and their headlines screamed out at me. In my work's canteen, radios blasted out even more details and people speculated about what else might be revealed.

Gradually the numbness that stifled my feelings lifted. Without its protective barrier, memories of beatings, canings, rapes, humiliation and acts of inexplicable cruelty filled my head. Those memories I had managed to suppress for so many years now demanded my thoughts.

Often, after I left that place, I asked myself why we had not gone for help – but where could we have gone? We didn't see the police or the welfare officials as our friends. Rather we saw them as being in cahoots with the authorities running the homes. So we kept quiet, not even talking to each other about what went on in those cellars. We kept it all locked deep within ourselves.

Now it seems that some brave souls did go to the police, and as the sheer number of their stories mounted up, some action had to be taken. I have mixed feelings about it. The wardens who abused me would be old now if they're still alive. I don't know what good the investigation will serve, apart from bringing up memories I'd rather have kept suppressed.

I can see him so clearly now – the other part of me, my younger self who was denied a childhood. For he still lives alongside the person I have grown to be.

He is a lanky, gangly boy, all knobbly knees and bony elbows; a boy who tried to be tough, a boy who wanted a home, who yearned for a place that was his; somewhere adults would look after him, care for him, love him; but of course that was never going to be his fate. His safety would only ever come from his adult self: the man who needs routine, who in the morning tucks his bedclothes tightly in and always washes up before he goes to bed.